Geoff Colvin
2585 Windsor Cir E
Eugene, OR 97405-1264

Living with Paradoxes

A Spiritual Approach

To Teri

In acknowledgment of your XXX birthday, you are an inspiration

Geoff C.

10/19/19

Living with Paradoxes

A Spiritual Approach

Geoff Colvin

Pat Foley

Foreword by Bingham Powell

Behavior Associates
Eugene, Oregon, U.S.A.

Printed in United States of America.

Living with Paradoxes: A Spiritual Approach

Published 2019

ISBN: 9781797519579

Published and distributed by:

Behavior Associates
2585 Windsor Circle East
Eugene, Oregon, 97405

541-915-1645
geoffcolvin@comcast.net

Cover designs and graphics: Kylee Lee

Layout, editing, and consultation: Mary Sharon Moore

Behavior
Associates

In loving memory of dear Satsuki Grace McMullen,
so deeply missed by her family and friends.
Geoff Colvin

In loving memory of my wife Jan,
whom I think of every day.
Pat Foley

CONTENTS

FOREWORD

In the circles I travel in, the word *paradox* is common. It is a word that conveys both energy and intrigue and we use it quite freely. Also, the word is often used to mean "end of conversation," as in, "Well, it's a paradox. Now let's stop delving into it." Like the theological word *mystery* and the expression "I'll pray about it," the rich paradoxes of our Christian spiritual tradition are too often used to *end dialogue*. In this helpful book, Geoff Colvin and Pat Foley challenge us to go deeper, to explore what a paradox is and how to use paradox not as an end to a conversation, but as the beginning. Even situations that do not initially seem to be about paradoxes uncover the underlying paradoxes at the heart of the matter.

As a parish priest, I find these issues at the heart of ministry: how to approach a serious illness or a loss; how to discern God's will for my life or, even more narrowly, in this particular situation; how to reconcile with someone who has wronged me. In these moments, faith and life so clearly meet, and yet we are often at a loss for how to take advantage of the moment, save for a few platitudes. Words often escape us in these moments because they should. We are taught from the great spiritual masters of our faith that only in contemplation, in silent prayer, can we learn to fully listen to the divine working in us and through us, and thus find our path through the paradox. This process enriches both our faith and our life, which ultimately are not separate, but one.

In these moments of paradox, the ground beneath us ruptures, opening up an opportunity to go deeper. Like a spelunker, we can go through the opening in the ground and discover majestic wonders. The journey can certainly be dangerous, risking our life—or at least life as we have known it—but the journey is also paradoxically life-giving, opening new truths and paths forward. Geoff and Pat serve as experienced guides as we take that deep spiritual dive into this cave, into ourselves, into the divine, into the paradox. By spiritually exploring the cavernous paradoxes within our own lives, we can find a place to encounter the essential paradoxes of Christian faith. I am so grateful that Geoff and Pat have offered us this resource to guide you as you encounter opportunities to explore paradoxes. They are not the first such guides, but much of the literature is too esoteric for me to recommend broadly in my pastoral work, making this a unique resource to help people enter into this journey. They have bridged theory and practice, helping to move us forward with courage and grace.

The Reverend R. Bingham Powell
Rector, St. Mary's Episcopal Church
Eugene, Oregon, U.S.A.

ACKNOWLEDGMENTS

We are grateful to our many friends and colleagues who took the time to read and respond to our initial article on paradoxes. Their thoughtful comments, questions, suggestions, and encouragement set the stage and direction for us to write this book. To this end we are most grateful to Bill Apel, Doug Carnine, Paul Davine, Alex Granzin, James Gunn, Rudy and Helen Hwa, Jody Irwin, Ed Kame'enui, Marilyn Nersesian, Vic O'Callaghan, Ken Paul, Nancy Roberts, Jim Somers, and Kerry Stirling.

In addition, another group of friends and colleagues took on the task of reviewing the first draft of our manuscript. These insightful reviews gave us helpful feedback on the content itself, the structure and flow of the book, and especially the usefulness of the material for potential seekers in developing and growing their own spiritual pathways. We wish to sincerely thank the following for their assistance and expertise in this review process: Pam Birrell, Jerry Braza, Anne Cottam, Sarah Foley Massa, Hillary

Kittleson, Guy Maynard, Marshal J. McMahon, Rev. Heather Parr, Ron Perry, Michael Seely, and Br. Roger Vallance.

We offer special acknowledgement to Guy Maynard for his meticulous and highly skillful editing of the manuscript and for his constructive responses to the overall intent of the book from his personal perspective. In addition, we gratefully acknowledge Ariana Sinclair for her systematic and thorough copyediting and helpful feedback.

We also express our sincere gratitude to Kylee Lee for her expertise in designing the book cover and especially in creating a graphic that so poignantly represents living with paradoxes.

Finally, we deeply acknowledge Mary Sharon Moore who has been an invaluable resource in helping us to get our manuscript into a publishable form. She has made significant contributions at every level including content, layout, and especially her skillful and detailed editing. We are very much indebted to her.

ABOUT THE COVER DESIGN

The spiral helix captures the sense of journey in the spiritual approach to living with paradoxes. The Greek prefix *para-* means *beyond.* The center represents the starting point where we are caught in a paradox.

While options to escape are evident, we do not know which one to choose; we experience a sense of being in a maze that leaves us anxious and confused. However, when we take a spiritual approach and turn the situation over to God, we begin to sense being led along a path that may provide hope and relief. Still, as we follow this path, we may feel that we are walking in circles. This sense of insecurity oftentimes reveals our reluctance to fully let go and trust in God's active presence and the invitation that God is offering us. As we gain confidence in God's way in this journey, we start to experience a feeling of emergence from our stuck point to a brighter, more open, and integrated solution, leading to fuller communion with God.

INTRODUCTION

Grace fills empty spaces,
but it can only enter where there is a void to receive it,
and it is grace itself which makes this void.

~Simone Weil[1]

How often have we heard friends, workmates, or relatives, with a certain anxiety and frustration, say things like …

- I don't know where to turn. I feel stuck.

- I am between a rock and a hard place. The choices I have don't work and I see no other course.

- I can usually work things out but I am in a no-man's land here for sure.

- It is like being in a new void. Nothing seems available that is workable.

- I feel a real tug. One part pulling me this way and another part pulling me that way.

- There is no shortage of suggestions as to what I am dealing with. The frustrating thing is that the suggestions contradict each other.

What we have here is a series of quite common life experiences. In fact, most people would say in response to these situations, "Yes. I've been there," or "That sounds like my story right now," or "I could easily add to the list."

The first author of this book, Geoff Colvin, addressed these very kinds of conflicts, voids, or quandaries that beset most people regularly in an article recently published in the Episcopal Café, titled *Living with Paradoxes: An Untapped Grace?*[2] While the feedback was quite positive, many friends and colleagues made several suggestions, with words of encouragement to take the material further. They wanted information on how to develop an essentially Christian approach to living with paradoxes. Geoff, with life-long friend and colleague Pat Foley, then set about to write *Living with Paradoxes*, with detail on how to include paradoxes as an integral part of the Christian spiritual pathway.

We believe that more is needed than simply pursuing strategies to find solutions, that is something more than a problem-solving approach. We offer a spiritual approach in which we explore ways to "live in" these situations wrought by paradoxes and see them as God's action in our lives. In this way, the voids and tension become a source of grace, an opportunity to trust in God at a deeper level, giving rise to a richer union with God. Sure, solutions to the problems may come, and we may pursue them. However, our message in *Living with Paradoxes* is to embrace the voids, as a gift from God, in a detached way so that our responses become more aligned with following the spiritual path laid out by Jesus, and not so much with what we think we need.

Before we address the various pieces involved in living in a void, we need to briefly clarify what we mean by void. Specifically, the term void can be applied to at least three quite different contexts. There are voids associated with the experience of (a) loss, (b) failure, and (c) uncertainty, which is the focus of *Living with Paradoxes*. While these voids overlap to some extent, we will briefly describe the differences between them so as to sharpen the meaning of how voids are used in this book.

In the first case, we are familiar with experiencing the void in our lives that comes with loss. Specifically, we feel discomfort and sometimes acute pain when something highly valued, constantly present in our lives, is suddenly lost or removed. This might be grief following the death of a family member or close friend; loss of employment; loss of one's home or property through natural disaster or theft; or the disruption associated with retirement or relocation. In each of these cases an integral part of our lives suddenly becomes absent. Something is missing that has always been there, leaving us hanging in a void or emptiness that can be deeply disquieting. While people may deal with these disruptions in various ways, a common approach is to obtain support, to allow time for healing, and to take measures to recover and move forward with our lives.

A second experience of void is associated with failure. We are well aware of the pressure in Western cultures to be successful, and when we are not successful, or encounter failure, we experience a "downer," with varying degrees of intensity and duration, depending on the situation. For example, a child may not be selected for a sports team or a part in a play; a college student may receive a failing grade; a business person may experience bankruptcy; a surgeon may lose a patient; a worker may be let go from employment; or a couple may believe their marriage is ended and file for divorce. In each of these cases the individuals have tried to be successful and have not succeeded in what they had set out to accomplish. This experience of failure can bring with it a sense of emptiness, a feeling of inadequacy, with nowhere to turn. Again, individuals find different ways to deal with failure, such as tapping their inner reserves and resilience; receive support from friends and family; or seek professional assistance or spiritual guidance.

The third kind of void, which is the focus of *Living with Paradoxes*, centers on the experience of struggling with uncertainty and confusion from being in unchartered territory. We are thrust out of our comfort zone, navigating awkward transitions, facing challenging decisions that involve competing alternatives, or trying to make sense of information that does not fit our current framework. In effect, we find ourselves in a kind of no-man's land, lost or floating as if in a void, that is to say, in a new level of awareness and consciousness.

We use the term *paradox* to link these unsettling experiences in our daily lives and shiw how they can provide opportunities for spiritual growth and increased union with God. The paradox is a construct that centers on this level of consciousness or void arising from situations that involve contradictions that imply hidden meanings. These hidden meanings can elevate our hearts and minds to God.

Living with Paradoxes develops around four chapters:

Chapter 1: *The Reality of Paradoxes* describes and defines how the term *paradox* will be used throughout the book. Instances of conflicting situations giving rise to voids will help to delineate the critical features of a paradox.

Chapter 2: *Taking A Spiritual Approach* introduces the various teachings by spiritual writers on how paradoxes can be an immeasurable source of grace and become part of the fabric of one's spiritual journey.

Chapter 3: *Key Supports in a Spiritual Approach* describes the critical components and practices of a Christian pathway that have particular relevance to living with paradoxes.

Chapter 4: *Developing a Plan* is the reality chapter as it addresses where the rubber hits the road. We lay out procedural steps with guidelines for incorporating paradoxes into the ebb and flow of our own spiritual path.

Each chapter opens with key points addressed in the chapter. For Scripture citations we use the biblical translation New Revised Standard Version throughout the book, unless otherwise specified.

Living with Paradoxes is designed primarily for 'every day seekers' desiring to deepen their spiritual practice by learning to live with paradoxes using a spiritual approach. The book is structured as self-help resource to facilitate personal use and adoption. It is also expected that the book would be a useful resource to professionals who are in positions of supporting others in their spiritual journey such as clergy, counselors, and spiritual directors and would be a helpful resource to those involved with adult education and parish renewal.

Finally, we took steps to ensure that *Living with Paradoxes* includes meaningful citations from several renowned spiritual writers on various aspects of living with paradoxes as an integral part of one's spiritual path. In this way we try to open gateways to this subject so readers can pursue the topics more fully if they so desire.

1

THE REALITY OF PARADOXES

By understanding how opposites are linked together, we can move to a higher level of awareness where paradoxes are not stone walls but rather are elegant forms of expression. Consciousness of paradox increases the power of the human mind.

~John Caris[1]

Key Points

- Clarifying the defining features of a paradox

- Seeing how paradoxes have become a useful literary form

- Recognizing that paradoxes are a common life experience

- Realizing the range of intensity from low level to quite serious paradoxes

- Understanding how many of life's problems can be described in terms of paradoxes

- Noting how paradoxes can give us deeper understanding of our problems

- Appreciating how the concept of paradox can capture the uncertainty and anxiety associated with many life problems

In Chapter 1 we clarify the concept of *paradox* to provide a framework for addressing the void we often experience arising from conflicting situations in our lives. To set the stage for describing paradoxes we will present four relatively common experiences people have that give rise to voids, tension, confusion, and possible suffering. The concept of paradoxes will then be delineated, followed by an explanation of these four identified experiences of paradoxes.

Common Experiences Giving Rise to Voids

The Void Following Meditation

An ongoing experience related to how we close our monthly contemplative prayer service at St. Mary's Episcopal Church in Eugene, Oregon, spawned this reflection. This service consists of a brief orientation followed by 90 minutes spent in silence, alternating between sitting meditation and walking meditation, and ending with a closing prayer. After the closing prayer, participants often stood around in an awkward silence with some brief exchanges as they left. We thought that the closing was too abrupt and needed some structure to ease the transition back to daily life. We decided on a brief discussion before the closing prayer. This additional step was announced during the orientation at the next meeting, with ten minutes or so allocated for discussion. Nobody participated in the discussion, and the same awkwardness followed the closing prayer. We then tried some reflective readings to improve the transition from silent meditation to exiting the meeting.

Participants still felt an abruptness following the closing prayer, and still had a sense of being in a no-man's land.

This experience of a new and different level of consciousness in exiting the meditation led us to reflect on other life experiences where we are left hanging, as in the feeling of powerlessness from having to wait until the tension or void passes, or the futility in trying to force a solution.

Whether or Not to Admit to a Relapse

A good friend mentioned that she and her mother concluded that they were alcoholics and made a pact to quit drinking. However, the daughter had a relapse and was confused over whether she should tell her mother of the relapse, and thereby disappoint her mother. Or, she wondered, should she keep it to herself and deal with it in her own private way? There was a clear conflict and tension between sharing something with her mother (as was her custom) or keeping it within the confines of her own heart and avoid disappointing her mother.

The Conflict in Connecting with a Convicted Murderer

Similarly, a dramatic incident occurred when another good friend shared that a buddy he grew up with was convicted and sentenced to prison for shooting and killing his son. Our friend was torn between whether he should write and reach out to his buddy in jail, or whether he should remain distant and avoid communicating any sense of condoning such a heinous crime.

Grandma's Dilemma in Offering Parenting Advice to Son

A fourth example arose in talking with a grandmother who had concerns about the way her son was disciplining his children. The grandparent was struggling with the tug of whether to intervene and share with her son some discipline practices she thought would be helpful, or stay out of the way and acknowledge that her adult son has the right and responsibility to bring up his children as he deems appropriate.

Each of these cases presents an uncomfortable tension and uncertainty around how to act because of the pull of factors in opposition to each other. Specifically, the questions become: What can I do to smooth out the transition from an extended period of silent meditation to interaction with others and resuming normal routines? Do I share my relapse with my mother, or do I avoid disappointing her and manage the relapse myself? Do I extend the hand of friendship and write to my friend in jail, or do I stay away and avoid any appearance of excusing the dreadful crime he had committed? And do I offer my son some suggestions on how to discipline his children who are unruly, or do I step aside?

Variations of these selected examples are common human experiences, as Parker Palmer, author, educator, and founder of the Center for Courage and Renewal, aptly notes:

> Contradiction, paradox, the tension of opposites: These have always been at the heart of my experience, and I think I am not alone. I am tugged one way and then the other. My beliefs and my actions often seem at odds. My strengths are sometimes cancelled by my weaknesses. My self, and the world around me seems more a study of dissonance than a harmony of the integrated whole.[2]

In reviewing the commonalties of these examples of "being stuck in no-man's land," along with many other illustrations shared by others, we soon found ourselves entering the realm of paradoxes. The concept of *paradox* seemed to capture these experiences of a very different and challenging level of consciousness. At this stage we present a description or working definition of the paradox concept that will be used throughout this book to capture these awkward and, at times, anxious moments of uncertainty, and begin the practice of looking further, and being open to seeing the "more" in these challenging moments.

A Description of the Essential Features of a Paradox

Paradox, like so many significant words that have profound meanings, gets overused and becomes synonymous with many other words and phrases such as contradiction, dilemma, contrary, opposite, conflicting choices, oxymoron, and insoluble situations.

For the purposes of this book we use *paradox* to mean centered in contradictions but with additional, hidden, and deeper meanings that go beyond simple contradictions.

To begin with, contradictions are typically described as two things, events, or situations that cannot be true or exist at the same time—for example, early or late. If you are early, then you can't be late, and vice versa. Other contradictions include hot or cold, rough or smooth, single or married, employed or unemployed, and so on. In effect, contradictions are associated with *polar opposites*.

Definition of Paradox

The term *paradox* has its roots in a *seeming* contradiction in the sense that a hidden meaning takes us outside our usual way of thinking and beyond the meaning within the contradiction. The ancient Greeks combined the prefix *para-* which means "beyond" or "outside of" with the verb *dokien* which means "to know," to form the word *paradoxos*. This combination, *paradoxes,* gave rise to the term *paradox* which means a statement or proposition that seems self-contradictory or even absurd but in reality expresses a *veiled truth*. Paradoxes, as such, are a common poetic or literary device and appear frequently in our everyday language, such as "hidden in plain sight," "thanks but no thanks," "I must be cruel to be kind," "he seems much more alive now that he is dead," and the Portuguese proverb, "God writes straight with crooked lines."

At this stage we define the construct of paradox in terms of two essential features:

1. The context is set in contradictions where at least two perspectives or options are clearly in opposition to each other.

2. A hidden truth or message goes beyond the face-value meaning of the contradictions.

Relating Our Four Experiences to the Concept of Paradox

Our four examples offered experiences in which individuals were cast into a state of uncertainty or found themselves in a void with no clear ways to respond. The options seemed in conflict with each other. We will now describe each of these incidents in terms of a paradox, with implications for how to proceed.

The Void Following Meditation

Meditation can be described as a journey inward. The steps typically involve establishing a degree of stillness of body and mind so that we can rest in the presence of God. This kind of centering involves letting go of thoughts and feelings, daily events, troubles, and joys to become more attentive to the presence and action of God within us. However, when we exit meditation, we are making an outward journey that involves attending to others, the environment, and the events of the day. In terms of a paradox, we cannot make an inward journey and an outward journey at the same time, as they are mutually exclusive. However, a hidden message may exist in the awkwardness of the transition. It could well be that we need to be more attentive to the presence of God in our outward journey and perhaps not so caught up with others and events of the day.

The meditation group came to realize that a gap or void in the transition from immersion in the privacy of meditation to reconnecting with others is inevitable. A shift of consciousness occurs in leaving the inner journey of meditation and entering the outward journey of regular daily living. We came to terms with the realization that we cannot accelerate this gap, preempt it, or remove it. It is part of the process. Since then we have come to accept that we need to rest in this hiatus, recognize it as an integral part of meditation, and allow it to run its course—and to become more cognizant of the need to be aware and responsive to the presence and action of God in all our daily events, activities, thoughts, and feelings.

Whether or Not to Admit to a Relapse

The friend who was recovering from alcoholism along with her mother and was conflicted over whether she should tell her mother of her recent relapse was concerned about disappointing her mother and perhaps shaking in her resolve to stay sober. Yet, if she didn't tell and tried to take care of the relapse herself, she would be withholding information she would usually share with her mother. Clearly the two choices were in opposition to each other. She couldn't have it both ways.

The hidden message in this paradox may well be that the daughter should examine the depth of her relationship with her mother. If she cannot admit to the relapse, then perhaps the relationship is not that strong. Moreover, if she holds things back from her mother, there could be a question of whether she holds things back from herself, or is not honest with herself. This lack of honesty could be a contributing factor to her relapse.

The Conflict in Connecting with a Convicted Murderer

The friend whose buddy was convicted and sentenced to prison for shooting and killing his son was torn between whether he should write and reach out to his buddy in jail or remain distant and avoid communicating any sense of condoning such a heinous crime. Again, he was caught in the middle, knowing that the two options are in opposition to each other. However, this paradox may also carry a hidden message. It could well be that our friend is being judgmental and needs to leave the judgment and punishment to the courts and to God. It may be that writing is instrumental in setting the stage for forgiveness. We know that God forgives, so why couldn't our friend forgive? Moreover, if the inmate experiences forgiveness by his friend, he may be more inclined to open up and receive God's forgiveness and steadfast love, and thereby forgive himself. So, by being caught in the middle, our friend may be drawn to a deeper understanding of the cycle of crime, punishment, and forgiveness.

Grandma's Dilemma in Offering Parenting Advice to Son

For the grandmother struggling with the way her son disciplined his children, should she intervene and suggest some discipline practices to her son, or simply stay out of the way and let her son bring up his children as he deems fit? Again, she can't have it both ways. She either steps in and offers advice to her son, or she stays out of the scenario. As with the earlier examples, the apparent conflict may have hidden or additional meaning, such as: maybe the son was resentful, did not approve of his mother's discipline practices when he was growing up, or perhaps his mother was overly judgmental with her grandchildren's behavior and always looking for problems. In other words, the tension arising from the situation may encourage the grandmother to look more deeply at what is going on with her relationship with her son and grandchildren.

The Paradox Panorama

For several centuries the paradox has been used as a literary device to describe baffling situations and, in a way, make sense of seemingly contradictory statements. Paradoxes are often used to interpret events that are contrary to common beliefs which can have the effect of leading us to a deeper understanding of the issues involved. Effectively, paradoxes have become a significant literary device describing a wide range of human experiences in literature, poetry, science, philosophy, and world religions. While we cannot discuss in any depth here the use of paradox in so many disciplines, we want to at least encourage seekers to explore the striking depth and scope of such uses. In a recent comprehensive team study of paradoxes, Wendy Smith, researcher, scholar, and author, notes:

> While dating back to ancient philosophy, only recently have organizational scholars started to explore paradox. Drawing from insights across disciplines including psychoanalysis and macro sociology, some provocative theorists urged researchers to take seriously the study of paradox and deepen understanding of plurality, tensions, and contradictions. Scholars responded. As paradox studies grow, new insights challenge foundational ideas, and raise questions around definitions, overlapping lenses, and varied research and managerial approaches. Alternative perspectives highlight divides while inviting complementary approaches … noting how the chapters in this handbook both engage these tensions, while expanding insight into the field.[3]

In *Living with Paradoxes,* we develop one such application. Specifically, when paradoxes become an integral part of our spiritual pathway, they can be transformed to become grace filled opportunities for spiritual growth.

2

TAKING A SPIRITUAL APPROACH

No part of me, not even my mind and tongue,
can get through to God without passing through
the clash of contraries.

~ Cyprian Smith[1]

Key Points

- Describing the common problem-solving approaches and typical levels of resolution

- Understanding the basis of the spiritual approach in embracing the paradoxes, turning them over to God, and living with the uncertainty

- Reflecting on the Scriptures to understand the spiritual approach more fully

- Reviewing spiritual writings on living with paradoxes

- Focusing on three particular pathways to more fully see how we can live with paradoxes: Meister Eckhart, *The Wayless Way;* Parker Palmer, *Standing in the Gap;* and Richard Rohr, *The Third Way*

- Examining how one renowned monk, scholar, writer, and inspiring exemplar—Thomas Merton—showed us what living with paradoxes looks like

It is reasonably safe to say that all of us experience paradoxes frequently throughout our lives. In this chapter we address the question of how we deal with such experiences; in particular, we will carefully examine the spiritual dimension afforded by these paradoxes. In some cases, we are able to use established problem-solving strategies that seem to work and remedy the conflicts. However, in many cases, we find ourselves stuck in situations that appear to be unsolvable, leaving us anxious and confused. In this context of having to face paradoxes we advocate a *spiritual approach*. To develop this approach, we describe: (a) common problem-solving strategies, and (b) a spiritual approach.

Common Problem-Solving Strategies

Paradoxes can leave us in uncomfortable situations that can cause ongoing tension, confusion, disruption, and suffering. Typically, in response to these challenges, we adopt strategies that are designed to reduce, alleviate, or remove this stress. In this approach the paradox is perceived to be the result of conflicting issues that can be sorted out and solved by using one or more of the following *problem-solving* strategies.

Prioritizing the Choices

This strategy reduces the paradox to choices or options that are mutually exclusive. An example would be a person in the throes of a dilemma over whether to take the next step in a relationship and seek marriage, or to remain single, enjoy the

14

relationship that is already in place, and maintain one's independence. The individual may talk to several people and decide to follow what feels right. Once the priorities are established, the individual decides one way or the other. In this example, the person cannot have it both ways: if marriage is the choice, then being single is not an option, and vice versa. In effect, the approach involves establishing priorities and then deciding one way or the other.

Finding a Balance

Some paradoxes are not mutually exclusive but can be perceived as a continuum in which the factors compete with each other. The solution lies not in choosing either/or but in finding a balance between the factors. For example, a person may experience conflict and tension over the paradox of time spent at work and time spent at home with family. Following a careful look at time spent at work and at home, this person may decide to leave work earlier on two or three days each week and create more activities on the weekend with family to increase quality time with them. In this way, a better balance between work and family is developed.

Making Concessions

Here a frequently occurring paradox involves two factors that at first glance are irreconcilable between groups or individuals, causing considerable tension and unrest. The solution in these cases usually involves honest dialogue between the two parties, leading to some level of agreement and understanding. The process typically involves compromise and negotiations with certain levels of give and take. For example, a couple may be in conflict in their marriage, with each party feeling they are in the right. However, following counseling, they both agree to make personal changes designed to please the other party or to allay their concerns.

We return to these problem-solving strategies in Chapter 4, Step 3, as one of the steps for developing a practice of living with paradoxes.

There are usually three levels of resolution in problem-solving strategies for managing the experience of paradoxes:

1. *Problem is solved:* The conflict or situation is resolved, resulting in the removal of the tension, enabling the individuals to move on with their lives in a healthy and constructive manner.

2. *Problem is partially solved:* The situation is resolved to some extent in that, while things may be better, a level of aggravation or disquiet still remains.

3. *Problem is not solved:* The situation is not resolved. The individuals still experience the same anxiety arising from the paradoxical situation, with added tension arising from having made a genuine effort to solve the problem without success. There is the sense of being stuck and not knowing where to turn.

We return to these problem-solving strategies and levels of resolution in Chapter 4 where we describe the steps for developing a practice of living with paradoxes.

While it would be highly desirable to think that most of our situations involving paradoxes could be resolved using problem-solving strategies, most of us find that this is not the case. One of the unique features of paradoxes is that polarizing choices do not lend themselves to easy resolution. This means that we are typically left hanging in a void with varying degrees of confusion and suffering. At this point, the usual approach is to use *coping strategies* that translate to: "If you can't change it, learn to live with it."

In some cases, when people experience ongoing unresolved contradictions, unfortunately, they use destructive or counterproductive practices to bring relief, albeit temporary. For example, people may resort to substance abuse leading to addictions, aggression, or withdrawal, to levels involving serious negative behavior, or escape by developing unhealthy obsessions such as pornography, gambling, or shopping and spending sprees. In these cases, the individuals may end up needing specialized assistance to deal with their maladaptive behavior as well as to address the underlying causes brought on by their paradoxical situations.

It is precisely here, in this context of unresolved paradoxical conflicts where nothing seems to work, that the *spiritual approach* can be followed. This pathway can be helpful in dealing with such conflicts and ensuing stress, and can bring about a personal transformation leading to a greater union with God.

Foundations of a Spiritual Approach

In contrast to problem-solving strategies, the spiritual approach introduces a whole new direction. Here we are encouraged to *live in* the paradox, to *embrace* the tension, to *accept* being out of one's comfort zone, and to see it as a *graced opportunity for fuller union with God.* So rather than putting all our energy into removing the uncertainty, as in the standard problem-solving approach, the spiritual way is to *rest in the uncertainty,* to see it as a call to a higher level of letting go and trusting in God. The emphasis is on developing a way of *being* and *experiencing,* and not so much on seeking to understand and solve a mental challenge. This is not to say understanding and solutions should not be sought out, but to encourage trust in the knowledge that God is speaking to us and that a "solution" to the paradox may come relatively soon, later, or not at all. The spiritual approach can transform our efforts to deal with paradoxes in a way that unites us more profoundly with God. We present here some foundational material to set the stage to explore some practical procedures in the next two chapters. This foundational material includes: (a) the Incarnation, (b) teachings from Scripture, (c) explanations from spiritual writers, and (d) the Thomas Merton exemplar.

The Incarnation

The Christian approach to living with paradoxes is predicated on the doctrine of the Incarnation which teaches that Jesus, the second person of the Blessed Trinity, is both *fully human* and *fully divine.* We have already identified the experience of paradoxes as something very human and universal. Jesus, by possessing our human nature, not only shares this experience with us, but also embodies it in its fullness, as Richard Rohr, a prolific modern day spiritual writer, teacher, Franciscan priest, retreat leader, and founder of the Center of Action and Contemplation, explains:

> Jesus, as the icon of Christ consciousness, (see I Corinthians 2:16) is the very template of total paradox: human yet Divine; heavenly yet earthly; physical yet spiritual; a male body yet a female soul; killed yet alive; powerless yet powerful; victim yet victor; failure yet redeemer; marginalized yet central; singular yet everyone; incarnate yet cosmic; nailed yet liberated.[2]

Moreover, Jesus, by also possessing the divine nature, transforms all things human to the domain of the Divine. Hence these unsettling periods which we experience from paradoxes become a real and vibrant part of God's action in our lives. Evelyn Underhill, mystic, and prominent English spiritual writer, poet and novelist, describes this divine transformation in a way that brings us encouragement, hope, and trust:

> He takes in all the darkness and anxiety of our situation, whether social or personal; and within and beyond all, He finds the creative action of God, the one Reality, the one Life, working with a steadfast and unalterable love, sometimes by the direct action of circumstance and sometimes secretly within each soul

in prayer. And this creative action, so hidden and so penetrating, is the one thing that matters in human life.[3]

When we speak of "living with paradoxes" we suggest that once we feel trapped or lost in paradoxical voids, we turn them over to God as a *part* of ourselves. We see these situations as belonging to God's action in humanity, knowing that we need to embrace them, trusting that we will be drawn to a deeper oneness with the Divine. In other words, paradoxes, however challenging, can be seen as a grace enabling us to follow a rich spiritual pathway made possible by the incarnate Jesus.

Teachings from Scripture

Much of the teachings of Jesus are expressed in paradox form. However, we may assume that the intent in using this literary form was not to confuse us but to challenge our current values to show a deeper meaning. For example, Jesus said: "Those who find their life will lose it, and those who lose their life for my sake will find it. (Matthew 10:39)

This teaching is clearly a paradox in that if you have found your life it is not lost and if you lose your life it is not found. The contradiction is plainly evident. However, we are being led to deeper thinking in order to see deeper meanings. The challenge lies in questioning our priorities. Perhaps we are too consumed by the pursuit of material goods, fame, pleasure, or other transient goals. We think that when we make such gains we will have found "life" or happiness. However, our experience tells us that when we achieve one such gain, we are not satisfied. We then devote our time and energy to seeking another, and so on. "Finding our life," meaning achieving these temporary goals, only makes us desire more. Our lives can become consumed with pursuit of these goals, which never bring satisfaction no matter how successful we may be in achieving them. In this way we have "lost our lives."

Most importantly, Jesus not only challenges us to question these temporal pursuits, he is giving us the way and the motivation for alternative pursuits when he adds *"for my sake."* Here we are invited to follow the path of his teachings, giving us the fullness of life in becoming one with God. In this way, we "lose our life" by letting go of transitory quests and committing to a lifestyle based on his teachings, and "find our life," resulting in deeper, richer, and lasting freedom and contentment.

Jesus also uses paradoxes to challenge us at the very core of our cultural norms. For example:

> You have heard that it was said, you shall love your neighbor and hate your enemy. But I say to you, love your enemies and pray for those who persecute you, so that you may be sons of your Father who is in heaven. (Matthew 5:43-48)

In a similar vein, the Beatitudes (Matthew 5:2-12), perhaps the most seminal of all of Jesus' teachings on the Christian way of life, are replete with paradoxes. The use of paradoxes in Jesus' teachings is found extensively throughout the Gospel narratives. In addition, both the Old Testament and New Testament are rich with paradoxical writing as illustrated in the following citations.

Paradoxes in Scripture

Old Testament

How long, O Lord? Will you forget me forever? (Psalm 13:1)

Who is like the Lord our God who sits seated on high who looks far down [transcendence]. He raises the poor from the dust and lifts the needy from the dust heap [immanence]. (Psalm 113)

Some give freely, yet grow all the richer; others withhold what is due, and only suffer want. (Proverbs 11:24)

New Testament

But many who are first will be last and the last first. (Matthew 19:30)

So, the last will be first and the first last. (Matthew 20:16)

… but whoever wishes to be great among you must be your servant, and whoever wishes to be first among you must be your slave. (Matthew 20:26-28)

Give and it will be given to you. (Luke 6:38)
… and that you, having been set free from sin, have become slaves of righteousness. (Romans 6:18)

What you sow does not come to life unless it dies. (1 Cor 15:36)

For when I am weak, then I am strong. (2 Corinthians 12:10)

My brothers and sisters, whenever you face trials of any kind, consider it nothing but joy. (James 1:2)

Humble yourself before the Lord and he will exalt you. (James 4:10)

Descriptions by Spiritual Writers

Living with paradoxes has shaped the spiritual pathway for centuries. Noted Christian writers have given the practice different names such as:

The Wayless Way—Meister Eckhart

Standing in the Gap—Parker Palmer

The Third Way—Richard Rohr

The Wayless Way: Meister Eckhart, thirteenth-century German theologian, preacher, teacher, writer, head administrator of his Dominican Order, and mystic, used a paradoxical title for this spiritual pathway—*The Wayless Way*. Clearly, if the path is a *way* it is not *wayless* and if it is *wayless* it is not a *way*. Cyprian Smith, theologian, Eckhart scholar, author, and Benedictine monk, puts it this way:

> That is why we call the way taught by Eckhart the Way of Paradox, because it is founded on the tension between opposites. ... God and man, pleasure and pain, success and failure, are ultimately all one in God. But we cannot reach this perception, save in and through the tension of opposites.[4]

Meister Eckhart teaches us to understand God in a new way and to let go of the self-constructed images we have of God, as he writes:

> Nature teaches us, and it seems entirely right to me, that we must point to God by way of likeness, with this and that. Nevertheless, He is neither this nor that ...[5]

Eckhart centers his message on *detachment*, meaning that there needs to be a clear-cut loss of self in our path to union with God. Moreover, he teaches that the path itself can also become an attachment that needs to be let go, hence his expression *The Wayless Way.* Specifically, his instruction informs us that:

> For you to know God, in God's way, your knowing must become a pure unknowing, your knowing must become a complete unknowing, and a forgetting of yourself and all creatures. ... The eye with which I see God is the same with which God sees me. My eye and God's eye is one eye, and one sight, and one knowledge, and one love.[6]

Living with paradoxes, accepting the uncertainties, embracing the unknowing, can then be seen as compelling opportunities to forget ourselves and enter more fully into *The Wayless Way.*

Standing in the Gap: Parker Palmer has written extensively on subjects that continually challenge us to willingly enter unknown areas in our endeavors to pursue a spiritual path. In the context of paradoxes, he helps us to see that the contradictions—paradoxes in our lives—provide us with enriching opportunities to celebrate and respond to God's action. He writes:

> If we are to stand in the gap, we need to know the promise of paradox—and know it in a way that goes deeper than intellect, a way suggested by one of the most famous lines of biblical poetry: "the Word made flesh and dwelt among us."[7]

In addition to elevating our own lives when we accept the challenge to *stand in the gap*, Palmer teaches us that we also have the responsibility to accept our paradoxes, and thereby touch the lives of others:

> Standing in the gap is challenging, but the alternatives are irresponsible. ... But if we are willing to stand between the poles, refusing to fall out, we have a chance to play a life-giving role in the development of a child, a work-place, or a world that needs to grow into "the better angels of its nature." [8]

The Third Way: In a similar vein, Richard Rohr describes the spiritual path of living with paradoxes as "the transformative dance between attachment and detachment sometimes called the Third Way."[9] He explains the process of addressing two seeming contradictions in a way that uncovers a third reconciling or mediating perspective that creates a whole new level of practice. Cynthia Bourgeault, Episcopal priest, teacher, writer, and internationally acclaimed retreat leader, illustrates this progression with the well-known story of Jesus responding to the woman caught in adultery:

> When presented with the polarities of stoning the woman or freeing her, Jesus says, "Let the one among you who is without sin be the first to throw a stone at her" (John 8:7). He finds the thing that will put the terrible two binaries in a completely new relationship and creates a new kingdom ... called compassion and forgiveness.[10]

These very brief references to the works of these spiritual writers make clear that living with paradoxes is a particularly important dimension of our spiritual path. The essence seems to be that regardless of the conflict, tensions, and uncertainty, paradoxes bring what we need to accept and turn them over to God, to see them as opportunities to grow in our union with the Divine. Richard Rohr summarizes this transformation when he writes:

> Once we can stand in that third spacious way, neither directly fighting nor denying and fleeing, we are in the place of grace out of which genuine newness can come. This is where creativity and new forms of life and healing emerge.[11]

An Exemplar—Thomas Merton

It is helpful at this stage in our discussion of the spiritual path of living with paradoxes to take a close look at some aspects of the life of Thomas Merton. This Cistercian monk (1914-1968) was one of the most influential spiritual leaders of the previous century. His extensive writings, plus those of his followers, are still widely read and practiced by scholars and practitioners across denominations and religions.

Thomas Merton is a preeminent exemplar of how to live in paradoxes. He understood that paradoxes are an integral part of the human condition, and his life was no exception. As he said of himself:

> I had to accept the fact that my life is almost totally paradoxical. … I have become convinced that the very contradictions in my life are in some ways signs of God's mercy to me. … Paradoxically I have found peace because I have always been dissatisfied. My moments of depression and despair turn out to be renewals, new beginnings.[12]

He also showed us that we may solve some paradoxes but that others may be quite insoluble. In the latter cases, he understood that we need to live with them, see beyond them, and to be open-minded to what may emerge. He writes:

> Contradictions have always existed in the soul of man. But it is only when we prefer analysis to silence that they become a constant and insoluble problem. We are not meant to resolve all contradictions but to live with them and rise above them and see them in the light of exterior and objective values which make them trivial by comparison.[13]

The far-reaching writings of Merton, as well as those of Merton scholars and followers, abound with paradoxes that Merton faced throughout his relatively short life as a monk (27 years). The following list represents some of the deep-seated conflicts that Merton experienced, some of which were solved while others he simply had to live with as part of his vocation as a monk:

- To follow his vow of obedience, or to follow his conscience concerning world affairs

- To commit to Western spiritualities or Eastern spiritualities, or to both

- To keep his vow of stability, or to relocate to another community (or start his own)

- To honor his vow of celibacy, or to follow his heart concerning his intimate relationship with a nurse

- To live in solitude or to live in community

- To remain a solitary, or to become active in world affairs

- To live as a writer, or to engage in the standard life and work of the community

We cannot properly address each of these paradoxes here. However, we present a brief summary to illustrate how Merton experienced and dealt with three of these paradoxes.

Obedience or Conscience: Merton wrote publicly and with great passion, in opposition to the Vietnam War (all wars, in fact) and was ordered by his superior to stop writing on such topics. His letters capture the torment he experienced in trying to resolve this conflict and how he concluded that he needed to follow his superior's directives.

> Now here is the ax. For a long time I have been anticipating trouble with the higher Superiors and now I have it. The orders are, no more writing about peace. This is transparently arbitrary and uncomprehending, but doubtless I have to make the best of it. … But in substance I am being silenced on the subject of war and peace. … Now you will ask me: How do I reconcile obedience, true obedience (which is synonymous with love), with a situation like this? Shouldn't I just blast the whole thing wide open, or walk out, or tell them to jump in the lake? … I am where I am. I have freely chosen this state, and have freely chosen to stay in it when the possible change arose. … This means accepting such limitations as may be placed on me by authority, not merely because it is placed on me by authority, and not because I may or may not agree with the ostensible reasons why the limitations are imposed, but out of the love of God who is using these things to attain an end which I myself cannot at the moment see or comprehend.[14]

Eastern or Western Spirituality: It is well documented that Merton experienced a strong tug between Eastern and Western religions as well as related criticism from his confreres. Once again, he did not avoid the tension; rather, he entered into it fully, experiencing a deep unity from living with these unresolved differences. As Merton wrote in a paper which he intended to deliver in Calcutta in 1968 titled *Monastic Experience and East-West Dialogue:*

> [Third] there must be a scrupulous respect for important difference, where one no longer understands or agrees, this must be kept clear—without useless debate. There are differences that are not debatable, and it is a useless and silly temptation to try to argue them out. Let them be left intact until a moment of greater understanding.[15]

Celibacy or Intimacy: Similarly, Merton found himself deeply drawn to Nurse M (as identified in the Merton literature) during and following his hospital stay for surgery. Again, he immersed himself fully into the tension, experienced the pain of such immersion, terminated the relationship (thereby experiencing more pain), and continued his life journey as a monk. As he wrote himself:

> I got a very friendly and devoted nurse working on my compresses etc. and this livened things up considerably. In fact, we were getting perhaps too friendly by the time she went off on her Easter vacation. … I do feel a deep emotional need for feminine companionship and love, and seeing that I must irrevocably live without it ended by tearing me up more than the operation itself.[16]

There is no question that Thomas Merton's life was full of paradoxes. We are greatly indebted to him not only for his wealth of spiritual writings and insights, but also for his example in showing us how to live with paradoxes. He exemplified how to live with results where some conflicts are solved while many are not. He was able, in the confusion and suffering, to anchor himself in his vocation as a monk and to his underlying trust in God.

3

KEY SUPPORTS
IN A SPIRITUAL APPROACH

Make me to know your ways, O LORD;
teach me your paths.
Lead me in your truth, and teach me,
for you are the God of my salvation;
for you I wait all day long.
                                    ~Psalm 25:4-5

Key Points

- Seeing how we are called to follow a spiritual path, and supported by God's grace and action

- Identifying and describing eight key spiritual supports that assist us in pursuing a spiritual path

- Reviewing the basis for these eight supports in Scripture and spiritual writings

- Understanding how these supports give us resources for our spiritual approach to living with paradoxes

- Integrating our efforts in a spiritual approach to living with paradoxes by nurturing our spiritual pathways

- Realizing that paradoxes are a grace from God which provide us with an opportunity to grow in our spiritual lives

Our primary message thus far has been to encourage the practice of *living with paradoxes* as an integral part of a spiritual pathway. In this vein St. Paul teaches in his letter to the Philippians, "I can do all things through him who strengthens me" (Philippians 4:13). This means that the spiritual path is quite attainable as a gift from God and, in addition, we need to do our part. We must take up the challenge, knowing that God's grace and presence will support and lead us. So, when we let go of our paradoxes and other attachments and leave them with God, we are not bowing out. Rather, we are making them a part of a pathway toward a fervent willingness to respond to the ongoing action of God in our lives.

At this juncture we describe some of the underlying beliefs and practices, designated *spiritual supports,* that we consider fundamental to a spiritual approach to addressing paradoxes. Although people will implement and experience these supports in unique ways, we consider them to be essential components of a spiritual approach for dealing with paradoxes, as well as for living with the many challenges we face in our spiritual journey. We do not presume that this list is complete. Rather we have selected particular supports that bear directly on helping us to take a spiritual approach for living with paradoxes. Individuals may have found additional Christian practices which are helpful in following their Christian pathway. Clearly, these practices should be continued and, where appropriate, integrated with the spiritual supports we are describing.

We do not believe that these supports need to be in place before we can pursue a spiritual pathway. Rather, they are like the spokes in a wheel—they are all connected and contribute to the wheel's proper functioning. Moreover, we understand that the supports are *interactive.* That is, as one is developed, the others are enhanced. For example, as we pay more attention to *detachment* (Spiritual Support 5), we are more likely to experience a deeper sense of *compassion* (Spiritual Support 7). This list is not exhaustive but, hopefully, may suffice to provide a solid basis for building, shaping, and growing a spiritual practice.

Eight Spiritual Supports are briefly described, followed by their application to living with paradoxes:

Spiritual Supports

1. God's All-Encompassing Love

2. Contemplative Prayer

3. Nondualism

4. True-Self/False-Self

5. Detachment

6. Suffering

7. Compassion

8. Consent

Spiritual Support 1

GOD'S ALL-ENCOMPASSING LOVE

Typically, when we start to look at our Christian path to union with God, we focus on what *we need to do*. In other words, the route to following Jesus in a deeper way is to look at our levels of fidelity to his life and teachings and reflect on how we might do better. While there is no question that we can do better, if that is our initial focus then we are missing the point. The most fundamental of all spiritual supports needs to be centered on *God's love for us* and not on our efforts. This is to say, the underpinning for all our endeavors is recognizing and accepting God's all-encompassing love for us. To sharpen this focus of looking at God's love for us, it is helpful to reflect on Scripture, the revealed word of God. A dominant thread, in both the Old and New Testaments, is the message of God's *unlimited and profound love for us*:

> Know therefore that the LORD your God is God, the faithful God who maintains covenant loyalty with those who love him and keep his commandments, to a thousand generations. (Deuteronomy 7: 9)

> But you, O Lord, are a God merciful and gracious; slow to anger and abounding in steadfast love and faithfulness. (Psalms 86:15)

> Are not two sparrows sold for a penny? Yet not one of them will fall to the ground apart from your Father. And even the hairs of your head are all counted. So, do not be afraid; you are of more value than many sparrows. (Matthew 10: 29-31)

> As the Father has loved me, so I have loved you; abide in my love. (John 15:9)

But God, who is rich in mercy, out of the great love with which he loved us even when we were dead through our trespasses, made us alive together with Christ—by grace you have been saved. (Ephesians 2:4-5)

Humble yourselves therefore under the mighty hand of God, so that he may exalt you in due time. Cast all your anxiety on him, because he cares for you. (1 Peter 5:6-7)

So, we have known and believe the love that God has for us. God is love, and those who abide in love abide in God, and God abides in them. (1 John 4:16)

Understanding the word *love* in the context of God's love for us can present a daunting and perhaps confusing challenge. The reason is that the one word *love* has different meanings in a wide variety of contexts, so that the essential meaning can easily become lost or so diluted that it is meaningless. For example, we readily speak of love in relation to family members, sports teams, friends, music, natural wonders, food, pets, possessions, and so on. So, what does God's love for us, and our love for God mean, given this wide range of usage?

Christian writers have noted that ancient Greek manuscripts used different words to capture the various meanings of love, especially in commenting on human love and divine love. For example, C.S. Lewis, renowned British author and lay theologian in his classic treatise on love titled *The Four Loves: An Exploration of the Nature of Love*, describes four kinds love based on ancient Greek writings that have been reduced to one word *love* in today's Western usage. Specifically:

Storge: Affection Love

Phileo: Friendship Love

Eros: Romantic Love.

Agape: Divine Love. [1]

Similarly, Anders Nygren, Swedish Lutheran Bishop, author and theologian, in his scholarly work *Agape and Eros,*[2] traces the full range of nuances of the usage of the word love from ancient Greek writings to the present day.

The Greek term *Agape* for love is still widely used today in Christian writings and practices. At best, we can say that God's love for us, *agape*, transcends the purest understanding we may have of the word *love* as we reflect on his all-encompassing love which has been manifested to us in so many ways. For example, we have already noted the *Incarnation* in Chapter 2 where Jesus took on our humanity, embraced us, and embodied and defined a way of life in the reign of God. St. Paul continually reminds us in his letters of the *Divine Indwelling* and of the extent to which, through this love, we may become one with God. "It is no longer I who live, but it is Christ who lives in me," Paul writes (Galatians 2:20). Paul also assures us that God's love is always present—it is *steadfast*:

> For I am convinced that neither death, nor life, nor angels, nor rulers, nor things present, nor things to come, nor powers, nor height, nor depth, nor anything else in all creation, will be able to separate us from the love of God in Christ Jesus our Lord. (Romans 8:38-39)

Thomas Keating, Trappist monk, founder of Contemplative Outreach, renowned teacher, leader of contemplative prayer, and author of extensive writings on Centering Prayer, summarizes the far-reaching and ever-present love God has for us when he teaches us that God's love is at the very center of our spiritual path:

> The start, middle, and end of the spiritual journey is the conviction that God is always present. … Thus the fundamental theological principle of the spiritual journey is the divine indwelling. The Trinity is present within us as the source of our being at every level. Each level of our life—from the most physical to the most spiritual—is sustained by the divine presence. … The Divine Indwelling of the Holy Trinity is a truth of faith that is easily forgotten or avoided. Yet it is the one on which a radical personal conversion depends.[3]

Application to Living with Paradoxes
Spiritual Support 1: God's All-Encompassing Love

The central step in developing a spiritual approach to living with paradoxes is to turn them over to God. In this way we embrace all that comes with the effects of paradoxes in our lives, and we offer them to God as part of ourselves and treat them as a graced opportunity for growth in union with God. However, to do this we must have an understanding, appreciation, and trust of God's all-encompassing love for us. This love begets a trust in the Divine that enables us to live with the uncertainty and vulnerability that arises when we turn our experiences of paradoxes over to God.

Spiritual Support 2

CONTEMPLATIVE PRAYER

The practice of prayer, in its various forms, lies at the core of all major religions and spiritual traditions. For example, zazen (sitting meditation) is central to the Buddhist way of life; prayer is one of the Five Pillars of Islamic Practice; chanting of mantras is an integral practice of Hindu religion; praying three times daily from the Jewish prayer book, *siddur,* is recommended in Judaism; and in Roman Catholic and Anglican churches the hours of the day are marked by communal praying of psalms and Scripture readings.

Karl Rahner, German Jesuit priest, theologian, spiritual scholar and author, in writing on prayer with profound simplicity, said, "In prayer we open our hearts to God."[4] Many forms of prayer can be loosely grouped as communal or private. One of the most common forms of the communal type is liturgical worship a centerpiece of many religions. Typically, members gather, guided by a priest or church leader in a designated prayer center, such as a church, temple, or mosque, for worship of a formal nature. Common examples include the Mass, Eucharistic services, and other sacred rituals.

A wide range of personal or private prayer practices include meditation, either in small groups or individually; retreats; connecting mindfully with nature, music, and art; and mindful living or living in the presence of God.

We make no suggestion as to which prayer form is better. Prayer is a such a personal matter, and Christians usually have preferences in how they pray that typically involve a combination of prayer forms that are community and individually based.

We suggest that one form of prayer, the practice of *contemplation,* assumes particular relevance regarding living with paradoxes. Contemplative prayer focuses on our inward journey to rest in the presence of God who already resides at the center of our being. In contemplative prayer we try to open our hearts to receiving and responding to God's *all-encompassing love.* Contemplation, as a passive prayer form, involves an emptying out or letting go of our thoughts, feelings, and images, so that we can be open to God's action and his abiding presence. Ursula King, author and professor of theology and religious studies, expresses the paradox in contemplative prayer this way:

> The search for quiet contemplation produced the well-known formula *ne pensar nada*— "to think of nothing"—and thereby to attend to the All.[5]

In letting go of thoughts and our own agendas, we assume a position of waiting, trusting, and simply resting in the presence of the Divine Indwelling. In addition, we ready ourselves to respond to God's action that may take us beyond our present level of thinking and understanding. As David Allen, psychiatrist, cocaine addiction specialist, and spiritual author, explains:

> Contemplation is the awareness of God that takes us beyond all dualistic thinking, and which allows us to find ourselves alone with the Alone.[6]

In general, the practice of contemplative prayer typically involves four qualities—Silence, Presence, Attention, and Assent—which we will consider briefly here.

1. **Silence.** In silence and stillness, we are able to enter the center of our being, rest in the presence of God, and allow God to speak to us. Thomas Keating writes: "Silence is God's first language; everything else is a poor translation."[7]

2. **Presence.** Contemplative prayer has its roots in the fundamental belief of God's presence in us and our presence in God. It is an experience of *oneness* with the Divine in us, in others, and in all beings, as Thomas Merton teaches: "Contemplation is a mystery in which God reveals Himself as the very center of our most intimate self."[8]

3. **Attention.** As we become more attuned to the presence of God, we may experience an inner awakening, a growing awareness of the hand of God reaching out to us. Simone Weil, twentieth century philosopher, activist, and mystic writes: "Absolutely unmixed attention is prayer."[9]

4. **Assent**. In becoming more attuned to the belief and trust in the Divine Indwelling, we may sense movement we can call Grace, God's will, or an invitation to the call of God. Our prayer is a response of *assent*—to follow the call.

Australian Trappist monk, author, and international retreat leader, Michael Casey, writes: "We do not produce prayer. We allow prayer to act."[10]

Being taken *beyond* our present mindset and resting in the presence of God in contemplative prayer enables us to more effectively understand and live with the paradoxes in our lives, as Richard Rohr teaches us:

> We need contemplative practices to loosen our egoic attachment to certainty and retrain our minds to understand the wisdom of paradox.[11]

Application to Living with Paradoxes
Spiritual Support 2: Contemplative Prayer

The pressing paradoxes in our lives likely will emerge in our thoughts as we engage in the practice of contemplative prayer. When this happens, it is important to let go of these thoughts and turn them over to God. Moreover, in letting go of any thoughts and feelings, regardless of the subject, during contemplative prayer we are developing a practice of emptying our minds that readies us to let go of thoughts and feelings related to paradoxes.

Contemplation also disposes us to respond to the action of God within that may occur when we turn our paradoxes over to God. The shift in focus from our own concerns to centering our attention on God already within us helps us to let go of the concerns related to paradoxes and to turn them over to God.

Spiritual Support 3
NONDUALISM

Dualism, coming from the Latin word *duo* meaning two, is a common way of thinking that reduces concepts to two opposing elements or principles. In dualistic thinking reality is perceived in terms of two irreducible elements, such as comparisons, classifications, divisions, separations, oppositions, and differentiation (for example: good/evil; intelligent/stupid; knowledgeable/ignorant; rich/poor).

The dualistic approach, however, falls short when it comes to more abstract concepts that are part of the human experience such as mystery, suffering, God, love, and grace. These elements cannot be reduced to black or white concepts, to this-or-that, or to either/or categories. In these cases, we need to move to *nondualistic* thinking that can transcend separation and focus on the oneness, unity, convergence, integration, wholeness, and openness regarding the subjects considered. *Nondualism* then, as the term suggests, means *not two* but *one*. It emphasizes a perception of reality that is undivided and not delineated into parts, and that highlights commonalities and unifying features.

Eastern religions, especially Hinduism and Buddhism, have used nondualism in their teachings for millennia. Some pockets of Christianity, particularly mystics, have also used a nondualistic approach in writing about prayer and contemplation for several centuries. However, Christendom, and Western thought in general, has been predominantly anchored in dualism to explain reality.

There has been a strong movement in the 20th and 21st centuries from several Christian teachers, writers, and retreat leaders such as Evelyn Underhill, Thomas Merton, Henri Nouwen, Beatrice Bruteau, Thomas Keating, Richard Rohr, and Cynthia Bourgeault in bringing *nondualistic* or unitive thinking to the spiritual practices for the Christians of today. For example, nondualistic or unitive thinking helps to dispel the thinking of God not as someone separate from us, or some "super being out there" who protects us, judges us, and serves as a wonderful father figure and friend. Rather, to see God as someone who dwells within each one of us and the universe, forming a oneness and communion at the very deepest level of our being. In sum, Cynthia Bourgeault explains:

> "Dualistic" thinking is thinking marked by a rigorous "either/or" dichotomy and the insistence of black-and-white, exclusive solutions. "Nondual" is expressed in the capacity to hold the tension of opposites, rest comfortably in ambiguity, and resist the tendency to demonization and exclusion.[12]

Application to Living with Paradoxes
Spiritual Support 3: Nondualism

It is not much of a stretch, then, to see how nondualistic thinking becomes a vital tool for us to examine and enrich our understanding of paradoxes, and, in particular how we might live with our paradoxes as an active part of our spiritual pathway. While seemingly two-choice situations arise with nondualistic thinking, we allow ourselves to see *beyond* the conflicting options, and open our eyes to seeing a *oneness* with the two choices that seem to oppose each other. To live gracefully and well with paradoxes, we need to cultivate a nondualist mind.

Spiritual Support 4
TRUE SELF/FALSE SELF

The *true self/false self* has been a construct used in Eastern spiritual writings for centuries, particularly in Buddhism and Hinduism. More recently it has become prominent in Western Christianity, especially in regard to the practice of prayer and in following a spiritual pathway.

The *true self* is identified as the self that was made in the image and likeness of God (see Genesis 1: 27), and thereby realized fully when it becomes one with God. Thomas Merton, recognized as a leading proponent of the true self/false self paradigm in Christian literature, describes the *true self* when he writes:

> At the center of our being is a point of nothingness which is untouched by sin and by illusion, a point of pure truth, a point or spark which belongs entirely to God, which is never at our disposal, from which God disposes of our lives, which is inaccessible to the fantasies of our own mind or the brutalities of our own will. This little point of nothingness and of absolute poverty is the pure glory of God in us. ... It is like a pure diamond, blazing with the invisible light of heaven. It is in everybody, and if we could see these billions of points of light coming together in the face and blaze of a sun, that would make all the darkness and cruelty of life vanish completely.[13]

By contrast, the *false self* refers to the self that is identified with and limited to what is external such as events, possessions, career, pleasure, and accomplishments. Merton describes this false self in this way:

> Every one of us is shadowed by an illusory person: a false self.
> … My false and private self is the one who wants to exist outside
> the reach of God's will and God's love—outside of reality and
> outside of life. And such a life cannot help but be an illusion. We
> are not very good at recognizing illusions, least of all the ones
> we cherish about ourselves…[14]

Merton and other spiritual writers have been quick to point out that the false self is not necessarily detrimental. Rather, they say that it simply falls short in meeting our spiritual needs, especially when it is the only or predominant self we recognize. Michael Casey, in speaking of the false self, teaches that, "While self triumphs, prayer is impossible."[15]

Yet while our true self is defined by our oneness with God at the very center of our being, it does not mean we are isolated from others. From a spiritual standpoint, if all of us are one with God, then we would necessarily be one with each other.

In general, the simplest way to discriminate between true self and false self is to ask this question: "What is your center?" In the case of the true self, God is the center, whereas for the false self one's ego is the center.

The challenge for us then, as we travel our spiritual pathway, is to seek our *true self* and let go of our *false self* by consenting to the presence and action of God within us. Prominent nineteenth century Danish philosopher Søren Kierkegaard describes this transformation:

Becoming more of a self and more conscious of oneself is inextricably tied to becoming more conscious of God and vice versa: The more conception of God, the more self; the more self, the more conception of God.[16]

Application to Living with Paradoxes
Spiritual Support 4: True Self/False Self

Many of the paradoxes we face in our lives are caused by the influence of external factors associated with our false self. For example, we often find ourselves in paradoxical situations when we insist on getting our own way; when strong attachments or greed come into play; or when the need for affirmation or recognition becomes overriding. However, if we strive diligently to limit the workings of the false self and do what we can to cultivate our true self, we are in a much stronger position to let go of our paradoxes and turn them over to God.

Spiritual Support 5
DETACHMENT

Meister Eckhart, who is known by the title of "master," ranked detachment as the most important virtue of all when he writes:

> I have read many writings of pagan masters, and of the prophets, and of the Old and New Testaments, and have sought earnestly and with all diligence to discover which is the best and highest virtue whereby a man can chiefly and most firmly join himself to God. ... I find ... that only pure detachment surpasses all things, for all virtues have some regard to creatures, but detachment is free of all creatures.[17]

Regardless of whether or not detachment is the prime virtue, it is a crucial support in our spiritual pathway. Detachment, in its simplest form, means separation from anything that gets in the way of our pathway to union with God. In Meister Eckhart's words:

> Now you may ask what this detachment is that is so noble in itself. You should know that true detachment is nothing else but a mind that stands unmoved by all accidents of joy or sorrow, honor, shame, or disgrace, as a mountain of lead stands unmoved by a breath of wind. This immovable detachment brings a man into the greatest likeness of God.[18]

In effect, detachment does not allow us to be caught up in the inordinate pursuits of the *false self* such as material possessions, honor, accomplishments, fame, power, success, wealth, and physical needs or wants. It is not that these items are harmful in themselves. Rather, it is how we use them, and whether we allow them to consume us and obstruct our journey to oneness with God.

Scripture presents many reminders of the importance of detachment. For example, the very first Beatitude speaks to having a mindset of "poverty" in which we learn to live either without things or unattached to them: "Blessed are the poor in spirit," this Beatitude says, "for theirs is the kingdom of heaven" (Matthew 5:3). In a similar vein, St. Paul teaches the Christian community to not be overly concerned with things:

> Do not worry about anything, but in everything by prayer and supplication with thanksgiving let your requests be made known to God. And the peace of God, which surpasses all understanding, will guard your hearts and your minds in Christ Jesus. (Philippians 4:6-7)

In many avenues in our daily lives detachment can be and should be practiced. The drive we have to possess things, and the attractions which belong to the false self, all need to be tempered by developing a practice of *letting go*. As Jon Kabat-Zinn, founder of Center for Mindfulness in Medicine, creator of the Stress Reduction Clinic and prominent author, explains:

> Letting go means letting be. It does not mean pushing things away or forcing ourselves to release what we are clinging to, what we are most strongly attached to. On the contrary, letting go is akin to nonattachment, and in particular, nonattachment to outcome, when we are no longer grasping for what we want that we are already clinging to or what we simply *have* to have. ... When you let things be as they are, you are aligning yourself with that domain of awareness itself, pure awareness.[19]

In addition, Kabat-Zinn points out that we need to extend our practice of letting go to include the negative experiences in our lives:

> Letting go also means not clinging to what we most hate, what we have a huge aversion for. Aversion is just another form of attachment, a negative attachment. It has the energy of repulsion, but it is clinging just the same. When we purposefully cultivate an attitude of letting things be as they are, it signifies that you recognize that you are much bigger and more spacious than the voice that keeps saying "This cannot be happening," or "Things have to happen this way.[20]

The practice of letting go also applies as our spiritual path unfolds. Both Meister Eckhart and Thomas Merton warn us that as we undertake our spiritual path and commit to it fully, it may happen that we develop attachments to the path itself. Meister Eckhart used the name *Wayless Way*, to remind us that the path is not our own. We need to focus on responding to God's action and not try to control the path ourselves. Similarly, Thomas Merton, in writing on the contemplative life, said:

> Sometimes contemplatives think that the whole end and essence of their life is to be found in recollection and interior peace and the sense of the presence of God. They become attached to these things. ... Attachment to spiritual things is therefore just as much an attachment as inordinate love of anything else. The imperfection may be more hidden and more subtle: but from a certain point of view that only makes it all the more harmful because it is not so easy to recognize. And so many contemplatives never become great saints ... because they cling to the miserable little consolations that are given to beginners of the contemplative way.[21]

Hence the practice of detachment is a pivotal step in the development of our spiritual path. Spiritual writers repeatedly remind us that as detachment increases and attachments decrease, we become increasingly open and responsive to the loving action of God.

Etty Hillesum, Dutch author of confessional letters and diaries, imprisoned and executed by the Nazis in Auschitz in World War 11, gives us a profound reflection on detachment in one of the many deeply moving entries in her diary and letters:

> And now that I don't want to own anything anymore and am free, now I suddenly own everything, now my inner riches are immeasurable.[22]

Application to Living with Paradoxes
Spiritual Support 5: Detachment

In many respects, detachment is the key support for the spiritual approach to living with paradoxes. The reason is that the spiritual approach asks us to *let go* our paradoxes and turn them over to God, and then assent to God's action accordingly. This means we are exercising detachment at two levels. First, we need to let go or "let be" the paradoxes we are experiencing. Second, we are leaving ourselves open to whatever action God may manifest to us. We show detachment by consenting to God's action, whatever it may or may not be. In effect, detachment is a crucial support for our efforts to live with the paradoxes that come our way.

Spiritual Support 6
SUFFERING

Probably no subject triggers more contentious discussion about our perception of God than suffering. For example, we often hear questions and comments such as these:

- If God were so caring, how come he allows so much suffering in the world?

- If God were so loving, why is there so much evil all over the world?

- Why is it that the innocent suffer and the guilty are rewarded?

- Why us?

- We have done everything right as best we could.

- They deserve to suffer.

- We call it poetic justice.

Perhaps we have all had a friend or a relative who has experienced tragedy or excessive hardship in life, and have made the remark, "I can no longer believe in a personal God who would allow us to suffer so greatly." Like so many others, we would love to be able to write a few lines to clarify this mystery of the ongoing prevalence of suffering in the world and the abiding presence of God's love for us. We cannot and we do not intend to fumble along and try. However, the way we deal with suffering should be an important spiritual support in our pathway. As Dietrich Bonhoeffer, German pastor, theologian, and author, imprisoned and executed in World War II for his alleged anti-Nazi activities, in his letters from prison teaches us:

> May God in his mercy lead us through these times; but above all may he lead us to himself.[23]

The primary message here is that the important outcome from suffering is not so much relief but union with God. In a similar way, David Brooks, current affairs journalist and author, speaks to the idea that suffering is a powerful teacher in helping us to better understand what life is about, and that we need to make suffering a part of our spiritual journey:

> Suffering simultaneously reminds us of our finitude and pushes us to see life in the widest possible connections, which is where holiness dwells. Recovering from suffering is not like recovering from a disease. Many people don't come out healed; they come

out different. They crash through the logic of individual utility and behave paradoxically. Instead of recoiling from the sorts of loving commitments that often lead to suffering, they throw themselves more deeply into them. Even while experiencing the worst and most lacerating consequences, some people double down on vulnerability and become available to healing love. They hurl themselves deeper and more gratefully into their art, loved ones, and commitments. This way, suffering becomes a fearful gift, very different from that other gift, happiness, conventionally defined. The latter brings pleasure, but the former cultivates character.[24]

The role of suffering in our spiritual journey is emphasized time and time again in both the Old and New Testaments. Most of us think of Job when it comes to suffering. He is the exemplar of how to respond to suffering as someone who lived a blameless life yet was afflicted with prolonged and intense suffering. Yet, he was able to maintain his focus on God's steadfast love: "As long as my breath is in me, and the spirit of God is in my nostrils, my lips will not speak falsehood, and my tongue will not utter deceit" (Job 27:3-4).

Jesus taught us, through his own suffering and death on the cross, that it is not so much that we need to suffer; rather, we should try to accept or even embrace the suffering that comes to us. As Jesus said to Peter following the incident when Peter, in trying to defend Jesus, cut off the ear of the high priest's slave, "Put your sword back into its sheath. Am I not to drink the cup that the Father has given me?" (John 18:11). Similarly, the Apostle James tells us to believe that in accepting suffering we are paving the way to union with God:

> Whenever you face trials of any kind, consider it nothing but joy, because you know that the testing of your faith produces endurance; and let endurance have its full effect, so that you may be mature and complete, lacking in nothing. ... Blessed is anyone who endures temptation. Such a one has stood the test and will receive the crown of life that the Lord has promised to those who love him. (James 1: 2-12)

It is not that difficult to identify suffering in our own lives. Most of us can readily list a range of examples where we experience suffering, be it tragic losses, death of friends or family, physical setbacks from health issues (some more serious than others), pain, and the frequent aggravations in daily living. Suffering indeed is part of our lives, whether we like it or not. The real question is: How do we deal with suffering when it comes to us? Etty Hillesum writes in her diary from the concentration camp:

> The greatest cause of suffering in so many of our people is their utter lack of inner preparation, which makes them give up long before they even set foot in a camp.[25]

She goes on to explain that this inner preparation for dealing with suffering, even extreme suffering, is to focus, with resolve, on the Divine Indwelling:

> But one thing is becoming increasingly clear to me: that You cannot help us, that we must help You to help ourselves. And that is all we can manage these days and also all that really matters: that we safeguard that little piece of You, God in ourselves ... but we must help You and defend Your dwelling place within us to the last ... but believe me I shall always labor for You and remain faithful to You and I shall never drive You from my presence.[26]

In addition to finding strength from the Divine Indwelling to deal with suffering, spiritual writers also urge us to look beyond our suffering to the spots of beauty and comfort, however small, in our environment. For example, Dietrich Bonhoeffer, in the midst of extremely harsh conditions imposed by internment in a concentration camp, wrote in one of his letters:

> Spring is really coming now. You will have plenty to do in the garden. Here in the prison yard there is a thrush which sings beautifully in the morning, and now in the evening too. One is grateful for little things, and that is surely a gain. Goodbye for now.[27]

Suffering plays an important role in our spiritual path in preparing us to be of service and support for others—our ministry as it were. Twentieth century priest, teacher, and writer Henri Nouwen, in a particularly compelling book, *The Wounded Healer*, explains how Christ's life and death portray the vital relationship between suffering and healing. Nouwen then applies this paradigm to us whether in formal ministry or in simply reaching out to someone who is suffering:

> For the minister is called to recognize the sufferings of his time in his own heart and make that recognition the starting point of his service. Whether he tries to enter into a dislocated world, relate to a convulsive generation, or speak to a dying man, his service will not be perceived as authentic unless it comes from the heart wounded by the suffering about which he speaks.[28]

One thing we can be sure of—suffering abounds and it is part and parcel of *everyone's* life. We also struggle with trying to make sense of suffering and the prevalence of evil in the world. While we try to do what we can to alleviate the suffering, which may or may not bear results, we can also see it as a grace, something to draw us closer to God by including it in our spiritual path. Evelyn Underhill draws these thoughts together when she writes:

> Christianity shows us in the most august of all examples the violence of the clash between evil and the Holiness of God. It insists that the redemption of the world, defeating the evil that has infected it by the health-giving power of love—bringing in the Kingdom of God—is a spiritual task, in which we all are required to play a part. Once we realize this, we can accept— even though we cannot understand—the paradox that the world as we know it contains much that is evil; and yet, that its Creator is the one supreme Source and Object of the love that will triumph in the end.[29]

Application to Living with Paradoxes
Spiritual Support 6: Suffering

Suffering plays a critical role in how we manage and view the paradoxes we experience in our lives. Unquestionably, the uncertainty and anxiety that paradoxes bring induce a constant level of suffering that can gnaw away at our peace of mind. In Chapter 4 we develop a plan for turning our paradoxes over to God, which includes the suffering and discomfort we may endure. In this way our suffering becomes a grace-filled opportunity to strengthen us in our spiritual pathway.

Moreover, the more capacity we have for accepting the suffering that paradoxes bring, the more we can help and support others who may be suffering with their own paradoxes.

Spiritual Support 7
COMPASSION

Compassion, like many other spiritual supports identified in this chapter, has been a foundational teaching of many religions and spiritual traditions for centuries. For example, Confucius (551-479 BC), when asked which virtue should be practiced daily, said "Never do to others what you would not like them to do to you."[30] Similarly, *metta,* translated as "loving kindness," is a centuries old practice in Buddhism that emphasizes the unconditional love of all beings.

Moreover, compassion has been seen as an essential facet of the fabric of our humanity. Karen Armstrong, prominent British author and public speaker on comparative religion and spirituality, reports that the Council of Conscience, consisting of leaders from five major religions from almost every continent, adopted the following charter at their meeting in Geneva, in 2009:

> The principle of compassion lies at the heart of all religious, ethical, and spiritual traditions, calling us always to treat all others as we wish to be treated ourselves.[31]

The call to acts of compassion is not restricted to religious groups or spiritual traditions. It has been a common message from world and state leaders, simply because compassion cannot be separated from humanity. For example, a widely used refrain often heard during campaigns and public speeches, attributed to former President Theodore Roosevelt, captures the universal sense of compassion: "People don't care how much you know until they know how much you care."

In many ways Jesus' time on earth could be depicted as a life filled with *compassion*. The New Testament presents numerous examples in his ministry of his compassion for those who suffer, for example, his healing of a man with an unclean spirit (Mark1:25-27); healing the sick (Mark 1:29-32); cleansing a leper (Mark 1: 40- 44); feeding the five thousand (Luke 9: 11-17); healing a man with a demon (Mark 5: 1-10); weeping at the tomb of Lazarus (John 11:11-15); grieving over Jerusalem (Luke 19: 41-44); and giving sight to blind men (Matthew 20:34).

Jesus strongly emphasized in his teachings that we need to show compassion if we wish to follow in his footsteps. The parables of the Good Samaritan (Luke 10:25-37) and the Prodigal Son (Luke 15:11-32) illustrate how compassion is to be practiced. Jesus fully clarified the vital importance of compassion, or love, in our spiritual path when he talked with the Pharisees:

> When the Pharisees heard that he had silenced the Sadducees, they gathered together, and one of them, a lawyer, asked him a question to test him, "Teacher, which commandment in the law is the greatest?" He said to him, "You shall love the Lord your God with all your heart, and with all your soul, and with all your mind. This is the greatest and first commandment. And a second is like it, you shall love your neighbor as yourself. On these two

commandments hang all the law and the prophets." (Matthew 22: 34 – 40)

It is imperative, as we develop our spiritual path, to pay particular attention to including the practice of compassion—as we are reminded by the Evangelist John, "We love because he first loved us" (1 John 4:19).

So, what is compassion and what does it look like in action? Doug Carnine, author, Buddhist lay-minister and co-founder of the Spreading Kindness Campaign in Eugene, Oregon, links compassion to kindness in a three-step process: First, define compassion; second, desire to help; and third, take action:

> We can define compassion as sympathy for the pain and unhappiness of others, often combined with the desire to help. ... To be kind, we need not only to understand another's unhappiness and desire to relieve it, we must take action to intervene.[32]

As we develop and live our own spiritual pathway, we do well to examine the teachings of Simone Weil (1909-1943), French philosopher, mystic, activist, and spiritual writer. She worked side by side with laborers in factories to experience the hardships of the working class. She also suffered greatly herself with ill health, dying at the young age of 34. She reminds us of a critical perspective as we try to become more responsive to displaying compassion on our own journey:

> In true love it is not we who love the afflicted in God: it is God in us who loves them. When we are in affliction, it is God in us who loves those who wish us well. Compassion and gratitude

come down from God, and when they are exchanged in a glance, God is present at the point where the eyes of those who give and those who receive meet. ... That is why it comes about only through the agency of God.[33]

Application to Living with Paradoxes
Spiritual Support 7: Compassion

When we respond with compassion to people who are struggling with paradoxes, we bring the action of God to them. By doing so we not only support others who suffer, but we benefit in a way that helps us to live with our own paradoxes. We cannot be a vehicle for bringing God's action to others without bringing God's action to ourselves. Once we turn our own paradoxes over to God and respond to his action within us, we are in a much stronger position to provide compassionate support to others as they deal with their paradoxes. Compassion also helps us to understand both sides of the paradox, particularly in those situations where one party has been wronged or has done something "unforgivable." Compassion also sets the stage for us to live out the paradoxes associated with Jesus' challenging teaching to love our enemies.

Spiritual Support 8
CONSENT

Perhaps the most common theme throughout this book has been the reminder of *God's abiding presence and action within us.* We emphasize, in our pathway to union with God, the need to open our hearts, be attentive to God's message, and respond accordingly. In this final spiritual support, *consent*, we examine what it means to respond to God's action within each one of us. Thomas Merton highlighted the centrality of this consent in the spiritual journey during a retreat talk when he explains:

> There is something left in the depths of our being which is this yes to God. ... If we reflect and think, we sense that the whole meaning of our life consists in this yes to God.[34]

In describing Merton's "Yes to God," William Apel, author and professor of religious studies, eloquently points out how Merton's consent is so fully centered on Scripture, in particular the Gospel:

> Merton later told his retreatants that their "yes to God" had no currency without the gospel reality of a new life in Christ. This gospel changes everything. Nothing continues as it has been. All things are made new in the living Christ.[35]

When we examine Scripture, we discover the often-repeated exhortations to align our will with God's call, in both the Old and New Testaments. For example:

> Take delight in the LORD, and he will give you the desires of your heart. Commit your way to the LORD; trust in him, and he will act. (Psalm 37: 4-5)

> Trust in the LORD with all your heart, and do not rely on your own insight. In all your ways acknowledge him, and he will make straight your paths. (Proverbs 3: 5-6)

> Your kingdom come. Your will be done, on earth as it is in heaven. (Matthew 6:10)

Whoever does the will of God is my brother and sister and mother. (Mark 3:35)

Anyone who resolves to do the will of God will know whether the teaching is from God or whether I am speaking on my own. (John 7:17)

It is quite clear that to live a full Christian life we must draw on and single-mindedly live the message from Scripture to align our will with God's will. The step can pose quite a challenge to many seekers as there is something daunting or unnatural about "abandoning our will." Mary Sharon Moore, author, retreat leader, spiritual director, and parish renewal facilitator, in her writings offers a very positive spin on this issue by presenting God's will as an *invitation.* In this way, our consent becomes our openness and responsiveness to this invitation:

> The question, "Might you have an invitation for me," communicates to me as much as to the Lord that I am available, open to divine possibility, quite agreeable, even, to what God might have in mind, even though I may have no idea right now what these words mean.[36]

However, once we enter this pathway more fully, we soon come to realize that it is no easy matter to forego our own will, consent to the will of God, and be open and responsive to God's invitation. We soon become aware that many choices or decisions are not black and white. Our best intentions can easily become muddied with self-interest. We often experience the tug of not knowing what God's will is in many life situations. This confusion and challenge can simply arise from the basic belief that we have *free will* to begin with and that aligning our will with that of God is no simple matter. In fact, this confusion is probably a necessary part of the process of letting go of our own will and trusting in the will of God. Thomas Merton underscored these thoughts in his well-known prayer:

When the Road Ahead is in Darkness

My Lord God, I have no idea where I am going.
I do not see the road ahead of me.
I cannot know for certain where it will end.
Nor do I really know myself,
and the fact that I think that I am following your will
does not mean that I am actually doing so.
But I believe that the desire to please you does in fact please you.
And I hope that I have that desire in all that I am doing.
I hope that I will never do anything apart from that desire.
And I know that if I do this you will lead me by the right road
though I may know nothing about it.
Therefore, will I trust you always
though I may seem to be lost and in the shadow of death.
I will not fear, for you are ever with me,
and will never leave me to face my perils alone.[37]

The practice of consenting to God's will involves much more than a straight forward commitment or decision. To actually *live* God's will requires more than firm resolutions. No matter how daunting the challenges we may face, there are steps we can take to more fully open our hearts and minds in consenting to God's will that include: (1) show more resolve in following our Christian pathway; (2) understand the interface between God's will and our will; (3) develop a practice of discernment; (4) obtain spiritual direction; and (5) review daily.

1. **Show resolve in following our Christian pathway.** This whole chapter has focused on spiritual supports for establishing and maintaining a Christian pathway for our life's journey of union with God. If we pay vigilant attention to, and have humble trust in, the first seven spiritual supports, then we are more likely to be open to God's grace and consent to his will more fully. The first checklist in the next chapter provides reminders of the extent to which these spiritual supports are active in our spiritual path.

2. **Understand the interface between God's will and our will.** Often, we find ourselves caught in the paradox of not knowing which way to turn, and question whether or not we are following God's will or our own. If we believe it is our own will that we are following, then we may be moving off our Christian pathway, acting independently of God's grace. However, if we take the other extreme, sit back and "leave it all to God," thereby freeing ourselves entirely of any responsibilities, we could well be exhibiting *quietism* — a doctrine popular in the 17th century which proclaimed that the path to perfection was

to abandon all human faculties, sit back, and allow God to act in us.

The Christian way, however, is not so much an either/or situation regarding God's will or our will. Rather, it is knowing how our will can become aligned to God's will. That is, to understand that while God acts within us, we still need to respond accordingly. In addition, God can be seen working through us, and our response, thereby, becomes part of God's action in the world. Proverbs 16:1-3 notes "To humans belong the plans of the heart, but from the Lord comes the proper answer of the tongue." Henri Nouwen explains this interface clearly when he writes:

> Spiritual formation, to use the words of Elizabeth O'Connor …requires both a *journey inward* and a *journey outward.* The journey inward is to find the Christ dwelling within us. The journey outward is the journey to find the Christ dwelling among us and in the world. … These two journeys belong together and should never be separated.[38]

3. **Develop a practice of discernment.** The spiritual pathway is a journey in which we are consenting to the invitation, "In God we live and move and have our being" (Acts 17:28). While we are mindful that God is always present to us and speaking to us in many ways, we are faced with the challenge of knowing specifically what God is asking of us. Quite often several choices confront us and

we are uncertain which is the best choice to make. *Spiritual discernment* enables us to better understand what God may be asking of us. Nouwen defines spiritual discernment as follows:

> Discernment is a spiritual understanding and an experiential knowledge of how God is active in daily life that is acquired through disciplined spiritual practice. Discernment is faithful living and listening to God's love and direction so that we can fulfill our individual calling and shared mission.[39]

4. **Obtain spiritual direction.** Another way to find help in consenting to God's will in our lives is to take part in the practice of spiritual direction. Simply put, spiritual direction involves conversation with another person who allows us to explore our options, weigh the choices, review events, address our ups and downs, and reflect on related spiritual writings or recommendations, and so on. The spiritual director is typically trained and often is viewed as a teacher.

Some practitioners find spiritual direction through a more informal association such as communicating regularly with a friend, spiritual companion, or soul mate. In this way, a person may find clarification of ways of consenting to God's will through shared conversations.

5. **Conduct daily review.** Throughout the ages Christians have had the practice of a *daily examen*, in which one is encouraged to review events of the day in terms of fidelity to one's spiritual pathway. This practice enables the individual to discern the active presence of God in the course of the day; express gratitude for God's blessings, identify where we have been unmindful or neglectful, and humbly ask for God's action and grace for renewed resolve in the coming day.

In sum, this spiritual practice of consent to God's action must be seen first of all as a gratuitous gift from God, a grace, in which we are shown how God continually speaks to us at all levels, whether deep in our hearts and feelings, in events of the day, in joys and sorrows, our decisions, experiences in nature and the arts, and so on. Second, our consent includes the steps we take to follow through in living and growing in our Christian way of life.

Application to Living with Paradoxes
Spiritual Support 8: Consent

A critical first step in the spiritual approach to living with paradoxes is to turn them over to God. However, that is not the end of the story. The next critical step is to wait and be ready to *consent* to whatever God's action may require of us. We may feel drawn to respond this way or that way; or, no direction may be evident. Living with paradoxes involves consenting to the action of

God, in a trustful manner, which leaves us vulnerable yet peaceful in knowing that we are striving to align our will to the will of God.

4

DEVELOPING A PLAN

The human mind plans the way,
but the Lord directs the steps.

~ Proverbs 16:9

Key Points

- Seeing the need to plan for living with paradoxes

- Understanding that the root of our plan is to respond to the will of God, i.e., to God's invitation

- Recognizing that it is God's action within the heart that moves us to accept his invitation

- While plans are personal and will vary, four common steps are typically followed

- Completing the provided checklists and forms can be helpful to some seekers

- Seeing examples of completed checklists and forms that show what living with paradoxes means in reality

- Understanding that as we embrace living with paradoxes, we are embarking on a spiritual transformation

We have seen in Chapters 1 and 2 that paradoxes are a common human experience that can be short or long term, and can lead to varying degrees of anxiety and confusion. We also noted that some paradoxes can be addressed successfully at times by using problem solving strategies; at other times, the problems remain unresolved and can cause protracted perplexity and concern. While problem-solving approaches serve an important function, we advocate a *spiritual approach:* specifically, living with the paradoxes that come our way.

In this chapter we address what *living with paradoxes* looks like by examining more closely what is involved when we commit to a spiritual approach to addressing paradoxes. We are guided by the underlying belief that the spiritual approach requires us to see paradoxes as a gift or grace from God that provides us with an opportunity for spiritual transformation. Consequently, our approach involves turning the paradoxes over to God and doing our best to respond to God's action. While Divine action will vary in what it looks like and how it operates from individual to individual, we are comfortable in presenting some guidelines that may be helpful in *getting started* so that once we are underway, we may be more open and responsive to God's action, whatever form it may take. However, we are mindful that there is risk and uncertainty in taking these steps. In effect we are stepping out of our comfort zone to embrace the insecurity brought about by turning our paradoxes over to God's loving action. In this light, Manuela George-Izunwa, Rivers State Commissioner for Women's Affairs, Nigeria, and life-long advocate for women's rights, encourages us to:

> Sever the ties to your comfort zone.
> Stretch yourself to see the wonders for you beyond the horizons.
> Get up on your tiptoes.
> Reach up to the Lord.[1]

The guidelines we suggest for using a spiritual approach to living with paradoxes provide four levels of responses:

Response 1: Review relevance of spiritual supports in my pathway

Response 2: Develop an action plan to enhance the practice of my spiritual pathway

Response 3: Identify paradoxes of concern

Response 4: Develop a practice of living with paradoxes

Forms for each of these responses are provided to help you to develop a spiritual approach for addressing the paradoxes operating in your own life. A completed illustration is provided for each of these forms.

Response 1
Review Relevance of Spiritual Supports in My Pathway

The overall approach to living with paradoxes, along with the spiritual approach in general, should have its roots in your own spiritual path to union with God. Therefore, the first response to living with paradoxes is to review the relevance of the spiritual supports, described in Chapter 3, to your own spiritual path. The idea is that the paradoxes you are experiencing will then become an integral part of your spiritual journey.

The checklist shown in Table 1: Checklist for the Relevance of Spiritual Supports in My Pathway will help you to review the extent to which each spiritual support is present or active in your spiritual life. The checklist is followed by a completed illustration. Table 1 has the following structure:

Spiritual Support	Rating		
	Actively Present	Somewhat Present	Not Present

- The first column lists the *Spiritual Supports* 1 through 8.

- The second column presents a *Rating Scale* to assess the extent to which the respective spiritual supports are present in your pathway. You are encouraged to place a check in one of the boxes *Actively Present, Somewhat Present,* or

Not Present, to designate the level of presence for each of
the spiritual supports. Some of the spiritual supports may
be difficult or even presumptuous to quantify, such as the
first one, *God's All-Encompassing Love.* In these cases, the
checklist simply serves as a *reminder* of the importance of
this spiritual support and that you may need, for example,
to be more mindful of God's steadfast love.

• The third column, *Notes,* is designed to capture your
reflections on the rating results—for example, thoughts on
what may be happening regarding the particular spiritual
support, and what follow-up may be called for. A rating of
Actively Present would mean that whatever you are
presently doing should be continued. Ratings of *Somewhat
Present* or *Not Present* suggest you need to examine what
roadblocks may be inhibiting your particular spiritual
support and to take steps to enhance its practice in your
spiritual pathway.

• The *Date* is noted at the top of the checklist when the
checklist items have been completed.

The checklist will help you to pinpoint aspects of your spiritual
path that need attention. In addition, the checklist serves to identify
spiritual supports that may be relevant to a particular paradox. For
example, in the paradox noted in Chapter 2 of a grandparent caught
in the uncertainty on whether to intervene with her son's
management of his children or leave it alone and allow the issues
to continue, Spiritual Support 7, *Compassion,* may have some

relevance. In some cases, too, you may find that the concerns regarding a particular paradox may be lessened simply as a function of attending to your spiritual pathway without having to focus directly on the paradox of concern.

In general, the first response in the spiritual approach for living with paradoxes is to examine the level of presence of the listed spiritual supports in your spiritual pathway. The checklist may serve as a resource for making this determination and for guiding what steps need to be taken initially. The *Checklist for the Presence of the Spiritual Supports in My Pathway* is presented in Table 1, followed by a completed illustration.

Table 1
Checklist for Presence of the Spiritual Supports
in My Pathway

KEY
Actively Present:
Somewhat Present:
Not Present:
Date: _____

Spiritual Support	Rating		
	Actively Present	Somewhat Present	Not Present
1. God's All- Encompassing Love			
Notes:			

2. Contemplative Prayer			
Notes:			

3. Nondualism			
Notes:			

4. True Self/False Self			
Notes:			

5. Detachment			
Notes:			

6. Suffering			
Notes:			

7. Compassion			
Notes:			

8. Consent			
Notes:			

ILLUSTRATION
Table 1
Checklist for Presence of the Spiritual Supports
in My Pathway

KEY
Actively Present: *While still a work in progress, it is active*
Somewhat Present: *Awareness is there but action is limited*
Not Present: *Neither awareness nor action is present*
Date: March 15, 2019

Spiritual Support	Rating		
	Actively Present	Somewhat Present	Not Present
1. God's All- Encompassing Love		X	
Notes: *I believe in God's loving presence but my awareness is infrequent and is tied to big moments like birth of my first child; skiing in the Rockies; getting affirmation from others. I miss a lot of opportunities.*			
2. Contemplative Prayer			X
Notes: *I go for ages with no prayer and seem to pray most in times of need— sickness, accidents and moments of sheer joy. I need a routine for prayer. Perhaps I will look into this contemplative prayer thing.*			
3. Nondualism			X
Notes: *Never thought about this much. Don't like ambiguity. I like things black and white. A challenge for me to hold both sides of a paradox, let alone rest in God!*			
4. True Self/False Self			X
Notes: *Never heard of this. I'm sure my ego sits comfortably in my center. Not sure where to go with this Spiritual Practice.*			
5. Detachment			X

Notes:			
6. Suffering	X		
Notes: *I went to a high school called Holy Cross, and if there's been one Spiritual Practice which has been important to me it's been this one on suffering. I've always sensed the profound importance of suffering in human life tied in with the image of Jesus on the Cross. Certainly helped to get through the loss of my second child.*			
7. Compassion	X		
Notes: *I think I am a compassionate person. Often reach out to help others in need, contribute to many charities, etc. But my compassion has curiously not had much spiritual dimension. There is a challenge here with something that is already on track.*			
8. Consent			X
Notes: *I love Merton's prayer about the road in darkness ... speaks to me where I am. I need to consent to getting started with these Spiritual Practices.*			

Response 2
Develop Action Plan to Enhance the Practice of
My Spiritual Pathway

It may be that when you examine the extent to which the spiritual supports are operating in your pathway, in Table 1, you conclude that you have a long way to go in developing a solid practice. In fact, it is relatively easy to become discouraged, confused, or overwhelmed by where to start. This next step is designed to assist you in pinpointing where to start in shoring up your spiritual pathway based on the eight spiritual supports we have identified and to determine what actions you might take in developing a more committed practice.

You are invited to complete Table 2: Action Plan for Enhancing My Spiritual Pathway, comprised of three steps. **Step 1**: Select two to three Spiritual Supports that are of priority concern from the completed entries in Table 1. Typically, these items are chosen from the third option, *Not Present*, in the Rating column of Table 1.

Step 2: Specify what action you plan to take with this particular Spiritual Support. It is important to be specific, and it is equally important to choose actions that you can realistically implement. That is, do not get so ambitious that the actions are not likely to be completed nor sustained. Take small manageable steps that will lead to further steps and continued growth.

Step 3: Periodically review how the action plan is working or not working for you—say, every two to three weeks, and make adjustments as necessary. If you are reasonably satisfied that the particular spiritual support has become more regular in your practice, you may consider expanding the Spiritual Support or addressing other supports that you feel need attention, based on your entries in Table 1.

You are now invited to complete the blank form Table 2: Action Plan for Enhancing my Spiritual Pathway. A completed illustration follows this blank form for Table 2.

Table 2
Action Plan for Enhancing My Spiritual Pathway

Date: _____

Priority: Spiritual Support	Action Plan	Review Date

ILLUSTRATION
Table 2
Action Plan for Enhancing My Spiritual Pathway

Date: *March 27, 2019*

Priority: Spiritual Support	Action Plan	Review Date
Nondualism	*I have to let go and relax when things are not black and white.* *I must try to show patience and acceptance when decisions are not readily forthcoming.*	*May 7, 2019*
Detachment	*I need to try to simply express my opinions and not try so hard to convince others or to get them to agree with me.* *I have to work harder at not getting mad when I don't get my own way, especially with group decisions.*	*May 7, 2019*

Response 3
Identify Paradoxes of Concern

From the many people we talked to in writing *Living with Paradoxes* we discovered that the challenge of dealing with paradoxes was a very common experience. We also found a broad range in the *contexts* for these paradoxes. In this third response, you are invited to pinpoint the various paradoxes that are operating in your life. As a guide to identifying these paradoxes, Table 3 is structured around the different contexts where paradoxes are typically experienced. Essentially, you examine each context and ask questions such as:

- What gaps exist between what I would like to be present and what is actually present?

- What contradictions are present for me?

- Where do I feel I am living in the gap, wondering whether I should do this or that?

- What conflicts leave me stranded in a no-man's land?

Responses to these questions, and related questions, are then noted in the respective contexts in Table 3: Identifying Paradoxes for Specific Contexts, followed by an illustration.

Table 3
Identifying Paradoxes for Specific Contexts

SPECIFIC CONTEXTS

1. Self

2. Family

3. Friends

4. Work

5. Neighbors

6. Affiliations (church, social or civic groups, memberships)

7. Other

ILLUSTRATION

Table 3:

Identifying Paradoxes for Specific Contexts

SPECIFIC CONTEXTS

1. Self:

2. Family: *When I was an adolescent my mother died and my father remarried fairly soon afterwards. I never got on with my new stepmother (mainly because she did not do things like my mother) and I think she was jealous of me as a competitor for my father's affection. There were ongoing terrible rows. I left home as soon as I finished high school and have never returned. There has been no communication with my stepmother, although I catch up with my father from time to time. I feel in no-man's land with this matter and would like to resolve it somehow.*

3. Friends:

4. Work: *Years ago, a supervisor gave me a very hard time and actually had me unjustly dismissed from my job in such a way that I could not appeal the decision. I have not spoken to the person since but I hear now he is dying of cancer. I feel I should visit him and forgive him those wrongs from long ago, but there is still anger in me about what he did and I am not easily moved to make the move!*

5. Neighbors

6. Affiliations (church, social or civicgroups, and memberships): *A priest whom I regarded as a very good pastor and a friend of mine was found guilty on counts of child sex abuse and jailed. He had pleaded guilty at his trial. Such people these days seem to be beyond the pale ... beyond forgiveness! I feel I should at least visit him in jail, but then draw back because I may seem to be condoning what he did or to be showing disrespect for his victims. Quite a dilemma for sure.*

7. Other

Response 4
Develop a Practice of Living with Paradoxes

A constant theme throughout this book has been our need to respond more fully to the presence and action of God within us and in all things. In effect, we need constantly to turn our lives over to God. It may seem presumptuous to now address some steps that we can engage in to live this spiritual path. That is, if we turn all things over to God, how can we presume to delineate what we can do to facilitate such a "letting go?" In Chapter 3, the last spiritual practice, *Consent*, speaks to our willingness to act in accordance with God's action in our lives. The call is to *align* our will and not to *bury* it.

The fourth response, involving developing a practice, focuses on the steps we can take to align our will to God's will—that is to respond positively to God's invitation whatever it may be. Specifically, we list six action steps we can take to commit to the spiritual approach for *living with paradoxes:*

> Step 1: Select a paradox
>
> Step 2: Turn the problem over to God
>
> Step 3: Use problem solving strategies
>
> Step 4: Evaluate results
>
> Step 5: Determine next steps
>
> Step 6: Embrace the uncertainty

Step 1: Select a paradox

In the previous section of this chapter, we offered guidelines for identifying paradoxes that may be operative in your life. At this juncture you are asked to select one of these paradoxes that was listed in Table 2: Identifying Paradoxes for Specific Contexts. Because some items may have more weight than others, we suggest that you begin with a less complicated paradox so as to get familiar with the steps, and then proceed to a more challenging or worrisome paradoxes.

Step 2: Turn the problem over to God

A major goal in the spiritual pathway is to turn everything over to God, and by everything we mean little events and ordinary things, as well as troubles that include paradoxes, and of course, crisis situations. Even though a solution to a problem may readily be determined, or the events you are involved in do not "need God's help" as it were, you still leave them with God. Such a practice requires letting go, creating space, and most importantly, recognizing the presence of God in all things both small and highly significant. One challenge is to have a way of turning all things over to God. What does it look like? How do I do it? The most common strategy is to use a prayer form—either an actual favorite prayer or simply use your own words, such as:

Lord, I offer you this ...
Lord, I believe in your presence and wish to leave this ...
with you.
God, this moment is yours. I leave it with you and trust you.

An essential part of turning the concern over to God is to pause your thoughts on the matter, to wait, and then leave it with God. It may be helpful to leave it with God and simply engage in another activity as a way to let go of the concern. Most likely you will resume your thinking and perhaps continue to worry about the subject that you have just handed over to God. In these cases, you repeat the prayer wherein you offered the concern to God, then engage yourself in something else.

It is also helpful to express gratitude to God during these moments for all you have been given and for this particular experience with paradox. In this way you recognize the challenge to let go and turn things over to God as an opportunity for prayers of gratitude—a response to *God's All-Encompassing Love*—the heart of your spiritual path.

Step 3: Use Problem Solving Strategies

In Chapter 2 we described three broad strategies that are typically employed to address problems and concerns—in this case dealing with paradoxes:

1.   Prioritizing the choices

2.   Finding a balance

3.   Making concessions

Depending on the nature of the problem, you are encouraged to select and implement one of these approaches to address the identified paradox.

Step 4: Evaluate Results

We also described in Chapter 2 three levels of resolution which problem-solving interventions can produce:

1. Problem is solved

2. Problem is partially solved

3. Problem is not solved

You are now invited to make a determination on the level of resolution of the problem following the intervention.

Step 5: Determine Next Steps

Once the degree of effectiveness of the problem-solving intervention has been assessed, you determine a course of action based on these results.

Problem solved. Prayer of thanks is offered. Follow-up steps may be needed. Otherwise, move on with trying to live out your Christian pathway.

Problem partially solved. Prayer of thanks is offered. A decision is made to continue the plan with some modifications. It is also recommended to examine the eight Spiritual Supports to see if one or more needs to be addressed more fully.

Problem not solved. Prayer of thanks is offered. Here is where living with paradoxes comes more fully into play. It is here you grasp the paradox as fully as possible and turn it and yourself over to God. There is a oneness between God, the paradox, and you.

Step 6: Embrace the Uncertainty

A genuine effort has been made to resolve the paradox by traditional problem-solving methods, yet the problem has not been resolved. Now you fully embrace the paradox, turn it over to God once again, and commit to living with the uncertainty that may follow. The Merton prayer, *When the Road Ahead is in Darkness,* cited in Chapter 3, captures the commitment, mystery, and vulnerability you may experience in following this step. The attitude is that the paradox, with its accompanying uncertainty, discomfort, and perhaps suffering, is a grace sent to you by God. Your response or consent is to live with this situation and to see it as part of living in the presence and action of God. Should clarity on how to proceed eventually come, you act accordingly. If not, continue to live in the paradox. In this way paradoxes become a blessing or grace that leads you to a fuller union with God.

You are invited to complete the blank form, Table 4: Steps for Developing a Spiritual Approach for Addressing Paradoxes, for addressing the paradoxes operating in your life. A completed illustration for Table 4 is also presented.

Table 4
Steps for Developing a Spiritual Approach
to Address Paradoxes

Date: _____

STEP	NOTES & ACTION RESPONSE
1. Select paradox	
2. Turn problem over to God	

3. Use problem solving strategies:
 	
  a. Prioritizing the choices
  b. Finding a balance
  c. Making concessions	

4. Evaluate results:
 	
  a. Problem is solved
  b. Problem is partially solved
  c. Problem is not solved	

5. Determine next steps	
6. Embrace the uncertainty	

ILLUSTRATION
Table 4
Steps for Developing a Spiritual Approach
to Address Paradoxes

Date: February 21, 2019

STEP	NOTES & ACTION RESPONSE
1. Select paradox	*Should I make contact/visit priest convicted of pedophilia who was an old friend?*
2. Turn problem over to God	*I will recite this prayer morning and evening: "Lord of forgiveness, I believe in your love for all humankind and I turn my dilemma over to you. I pray for light and strength."*
3. Use problem solving strategies: a. Prioritizing the choices	*Possible choices are: Do nothing and leave it to God's mercy. Make contact through a mutual friend via mail/phone who visits him in jail. Visit him in jail.*
b. Finding a balance	*Balance is in middle choices.*
c. Making concessions	*Reach out in a small way at first, knowing I need to go further but start with what I can handle. Put a toe in the water!*

4. Evaluate results:
  a. Problem is solved
  b. Problem is partially
     solved
  c. Problem is not
     solved
	Problem is partially solved by making a start. I no longer feel in "no-man's land." By approaching a mutual friend, sending greetings and best wishes through him, and maybe suggesting a possible visit. Not a bold step but feeling my way. At least I have made a move.

5. Determine next steps	*The next step is to get a response from the mutual friend and, depending on that, decide about more formal communication or actually make a visit. The Spiritual Practice here to address may be compassion. Having placed my paradox in the hands of the all-loving God I can more readily say with Pope Francis: "Who am I to judge?"*
6. Embrace the uncertainty	*So, there is still uncertainty as to how this will pan out. I don't know how he will respond and I worry how I will handle his response. BUT I rest in the comfort of God's embrace and will live with my uncertainty, accepting that I may never be really comfortable with the situation.*

CLOSING REMARKS

The transition to the second half of life moves you from <u>either/or</u> *thinking to* <u>both/and</u> *thinking: the ability to increasingly live with paradox and mystery.*

~ Richard Rohr[1]

L*iving with Paradoxes* was spawned through the experience of four recent encounters that had the common feature of being in a no-man's land. Conflicts arose that centered on a contradiction for which there was no apparent solution. We concluded that these experiences were examples of paradoxes. We soon learned that such experiences were common occurrences for many people and, in many cases, can be quite troublesome. Typically, people used different forms of problem-solving approaches for dealing with these situations that met with varying degrees of success. However, the residual paradoxes, where resolution was not obtained, often led to unrest, discomfort, and confusion.

We then explored a *spiritual approach* to dealing with paradoxes. In this way we turn over to God the conflict, discomfort, and all the feelings that paradoxes bring. We are mindful, too, that the word paradox implies deeper meanings than what is inferred at first glance. These deeper meanings may, or may not, become more evident to us because the whole spiritual approach involves turning the situation over to God and trusting in divine presence and action. In effect, our awareness or consciousness of the situation may or may not be heightened through this act of offering the experience to God. Paradoxes, in a spiritual approach, become a source of grace, an opportunity to exercise detachment and grow in union with God.

However, the action of turning our paradoxes over to God is no simple matter. For example, it may seem unrealistic to simply let go and "leave it all to God." What is our role in the spiritual approach? Do we simply turn everything over to God and sit back and wait for God to "take care of things" for us? The challenge then is to integrate our own efforts with the action of God as best we can. There needs to be an interface between God's action and our consent.

We are reminded of an exchange between a novice and the Novice Master in a monastery (attributed to Thomas Merton when he was novice master). A novice asked, "So you'll be teaching us how to pray?" The novice master replied "I can't teach you how to pray but I can teach you how to get started." It is in this spirit that we offer our book *Living with Paradoxes*—as a resource that might help seekers to become more focused on getting started with the spiritual approach for managing the paradoxes in life. Even though our consent to God's action is important in dealing with paradoxes, we must never fail to recognize, as Thomas Merton writes, "The only one who can teach me to find God is God, Himself, alone."[2]

A major emphasis of this approach to paradoxes is that, first and foremost, we need to develop and sustain a spiritual pathway to God. Paradoxes, then, become a part of that path. We recommend addressing paradoxes not as a separate entity, but to be included in the journey of becoming one with God. This spiritual path has many interacting components. We described eight spiritual supports that are common elements of a spiritual path that we have gleaned from Scripture and several spiritual writers. We do not claim that this list is complete nor that our descriptions are fully adequate. Rather, we hope that what we have presented will enable seekers to examine their own practice and make changes as necessary to live a richer life in their journey. As St. Paul teaches, "It is no longer I who live, but it is Christ who lives in me" (Galatians 2:20).

The final point we want to make is that living with the experience of paradoxes is a grace—a gift from God. Paradoxes, with all their encumbrances, can become a gateway to experience more fully the presence and action of God in our lives. Granted, it is a challenge to accept that confusion and suffering are opportunities to grow and become more transformed in our spiritual path to union with God. When we let go of the paradoxes, and turn them over to God, we may experience in a more profound way, a transformation which helps us to follow the Christian way of life more faithfully. Paul Tillich (1886-1965), highly respected author, philosopher, and theologian, fully captures what we wish to say in closing by describing this transformation as the becoming of a *new being*:

> The new being is born in us, just when we least believe in it. It appears in remote corners of our souls which we have neglected for a long time. It opens up deep levels of our personality which had been shut out by old decisions and old exclusions. It shows a way where there was no way before. It liberates us from the tragedy of having to decide and having to exclude, because it is given before any decision. ... That is the first thing we must say about the new: it appears when and where it chooses. We cannot force it, and we cannot calculate it. Readiness is the only condition for it; and readiness means that the former things have become old. ...[3]

WORKS CITED

Introduction

1. Simone Weil, *Love in the Void: Where God Finds Us* (Walden, NY: Plough Publishing House, 2018), 75.

2. Geoff Colvin, *Living with Paradoxes: An Untapped Grace?* Café Magazine, December 2, 2017, https://www.episcopalcafe.com/living-with-paradoxes-an-untapped-grace (accessed April 16, 2019).

Chapter 1: The Reality of Paradoxes

1. John Caris, *Foundation for a New Consciousness : An Essay on Art, Science, and Meditation* (San Francisco, CA: Westgate House, 1987), 99.

2. Parker Palmer, *In the Belly of a Paradox: A Celebration of Contradictions in the Thought of Thomas Merton*, Pendle Hill Pamphlet 224 (Wallingford, PA: Pendle Hill, 1979), 5.

3. Wendy K. Smith, Marianne W. Lewis, Paula Jarzabkowski, and Ann Langley, *The Oxford Handbook of Organizational Paradox*, Abstract (London: Sage, 2017), 1.

Chapter 2: Taking a Spiritual Approach

1. Cyprian Smith, *The Way of Paradox: Spiritual Life as Taught by Meister Eckhart* (London, UK: Darton, Longman, & Todd, 1987), 27.

2. Richard Rohr, *A Spring Within Us: A Book of Daily Meditations* (Albuquerque, NM: CAC Publishing, 2016), 237.

3. Christopher L. Webber (Ed.), *Advent with Evelyn Underhill* (Harrisburg, PA: Morehouse Publishing, 2006), 24.

4. Cyprian Smith, *The Way of Paradox: Spiritual Life as Taught by Meister Eckhart* (London, UK: Darton, Longman, & Todd, 1987), 26.

5. Meister Eckhart, *The Complete Mystical Works of Meister Eckhart: Sermon 83*, translated and edited by M. O'C. Walshe (New York: The Crossroad Publishing Company, 2009), 408.

6. Ibid, *Sermon 4*, 55-61.

7. Parker J. Palmer, *The Promise of Paradox: A Celebration of Contradictions in the Christian Life* (San Francisco, CA: Jossey-Bass, 1980), xxxi.

8. Ibid, xxxi

9. Richard Rohr, *The Third Way*, Daily Reflections, Tuesday, June 28, 2016 (Albuquerque, NM: Center for Action and Contemplation).

10. Cynthia Bourgeault, *The Holy Trinity and the Law of Three: Discovering the Radical Truth at the Heart of Christianity* (Boulder, CO: Shambhala Publications, 2013), 16.

11. Richard Rohr, *The Third Way*, Daily Reflections, Tuesday, June 28, 2016 (Albuquerque, NM: Center for Action and Contemplation).

12. Thomas Merton, *First and Last Thoughts*. In Thomas P. McDonnell, (Ed.) *A Thomas Merton Reader* (New York: Doubleday, 1974), 16.

13. Thomas Merton, *Thoughts in Solitude*. (New York: Farrar, Straus, and Giroux, 1958), 80-81.

14. Thomas Merton, *Networking for Peace: The Struggle against War and Other Forms of Violence and Oppression*, Selected letters to James H. Forrest and Daniel Berrigan. In

William H. Shannon and Christine Bochen (Eds.), *Thomas Merton: A Life in Letters, The Essential Collection* (New York: HarperCollins, 2008), 253-255.

15. Thomas Merton, *Monastic Experience and East-West Dialogue*. In Naomi Burton, Brother Patrick Hart, and James Laughlin (Eds), *The Asian Journal of Thomas Merton* (New York: New Directions Publishing Corporation, 1968), 316.

16. Thomas Merton, *Learning to Love: Exploring Solitude and Freedom*. In David Oberson, *Eros as Koan: Thomas Merton, Monastic Life, Zen, and M.* (The Merton Seasonal: Quarterly Review, 42 [2], Summer, 2017), 25.

Chapter 3: Key Supports in a Spiritual Approach

1. C.S. Lewis, *The Four Loves: The Much Beloved Exploration of the Nature of Love* (Orlando, FL: Harcourt, 1960).

2. Anders Nygren, *Agape and Eros,* translated by Philip S. Watson (New York: Harper Torchbooks, 1969).

3. Thomas Keating, et al. *Fruits and Gifts of the Spirit* (New York: Lantern Books, 2007), 2-4.

4. Karl Rahner, *The Need and the Blessing of Prayer,* translated by Bruce W. Gillette (Collegeville, MN: Liturgical Press, 1997), 3.

5. Ursula King, *Christian Mystics: Their Lives and Legacies throughout the Ages* (Mahwah, NJ: HiddenSpring, 2001), 144.

6. David F. Allen, *Contemplation: Intimacy in a Distant World* (McLean, VA: Curtain Call Productions, 2004), 104.

7. Thomas Keating, *Invitation to Love: The Way of Christian Contemplation* (New York: Continuum, 2009), 90.

8. Thomas Merton, *The New Man* (New York: Farrar, Straus, and Giroux, 1961), 19.

9. Simone Weil, *Gravity and Grace* (Abingdon-on-Thames, U.K.: Routledge Classics, 2002), 117.

10. Michael Casey, *Toward God* (Liguori, MO: Liguori Publications, 1989), 33.

11. Richard Rohr, *Faith and Belief: Waiting with Patience,* Daily Reflections, July 21, 2017 (Albuquerque, NM: Center for Action and Contemplation).

12. Cynthia Bourgeault, *The Heart of Centering Prayer: Nondual Christianity in Theory and Practice* (Boulder, CO: Shambhala Publications, 2016), 44.

13. Thomas Merton, *Conjectures of a Guilty Bystander* (New York: Doubleday: 1965), 158.

14. Thomas Merton, *New Seeds of Contemplation* (New York: New Directions, 1961), 34.

15. Michael Casey, *Toward God: The Ancient Wisdom of Western Prayer* (Liguori, MO: Liguori Publications, 1996), 15.

16. Meister Eckhart, *The Complete Mystical Works of Meister Eckhart, Sermon IV On Detachment,* translated and edited by M. O'C. Walshe (New York: The Crossroad Publishing Company, 2009) 566.

17. Søren Kierkegaard, *The Sickness unto Death: A Christian Psychological Exposition for Upbuilding and Awakening,* translated by H. V. Hong and E. H. Hong (Princeton, NJ: Princeton University Press, 1983), 129.

18. Meister Eckhart, *The Complete Mystical Works of Meister Eckhart, Sermon IV On Detachment,* translated and edited by M. O'C. Walshe (New York: The Crossroad Publishing Company, 2009) 566.

19. Ibid, 568– 569.

20. Jon Kabat-Zinn, *Mindfulness for Beginners: Reclaiming the Present Moment—and Your Life* (Boulder, CO: Sounds True, 2012), 132-133.

21. Ibid, 132.

22. Thomas Merton, *New Seeds of Contemplation* (New York: New Directions, 1961), 205-206.

23. Etty Hillesum, *An Interrupted Life: The Diaries, 1941-1943, and Letters from Westerbrook,* translated by Arnold J. Pomerans (New York: Holt, 1996), 16.

24. Dietrich Bonhoeffer, *Letters and Papers from Prison* (New York: The MacMillan Company, 1967), 194.

25. David Brooks, *The Road to Character* (New York: Random House, 2015), 95-96.

26. Etty Hillesum, *An Interrupted Life: The Diaries, 1941-1943, and Letters from Westerbrook,* translated by Arnold J. Pomerans (New York: Holt, 1996),183.

27. Ibid, 178.

28. Dietrich Bonhoeffer, *Letters and Papers from Prison* (New York: The MacMillan Company, 1967)*,* 19.

29. Henri J. M. Nouwen, *The Wounded Healer* (New York: Double Day, 1979), xvi.

30. Evelyn Underhill, *The Spiritual Life: Four Broadcast Talks* (Mansfield Centre, CT: Martino Publishing, 2013), 125-126.

31. Confucius, *The Analects of Confucius,* translated and annotated by Arthur Waley (New York: Vintage, 1989), 15-23.

32. Karen Armstrong, *Twelve Steps to a Compassionate Life* (New York: Alfred A. Knoph, 2010), 6.

33. Doug Carnine, *How Love Wins: The Power of Mindful Kindness* (Eugene, OR: Doug Carnine, 2017), 9-10.

34. Simone Weil, *Waiting for God* (New York: Harper Perennial Modern Classics, 2009), 93-94.

35. Thomas Merton, *The Springs of Contemplation: A Retreat at the Abbey of Gethsemani*, edited by Jane Marie Richardson, SL (New York: Farrar, Straus, and Giroux, 1992), 262.

36. William Apel, "This Yes to God": The Gospel Wisdom of Thomas Merton. *The Merton Seasonal: A Quarterly Review*, 38,4 (Winter 2013), 24.

37. Mary Sharon Moore, *Lord, Teach Us to Pray: An Intimate Look into a Maturing Prayer Life* (Eugene, OR: Awakening Vocations, 2017), 92.

38. Thomas Merton, *Thoughts in Solitude* (New York: Farrar, Straus, and Giroux, 1978), 83.

39. Henri Nouwen, *Spiritual Formation: Following the Movements of the Spirit* (London: Society for Promoting Christian Knowledge, 2011), 123.

40. Henri Nouwen, *Discernment: Reading the Signs of Daily Life* (New York: HarperOne, 2013), 3.

Chapter 4: Developing a Plan

1. Manuela George-Izunwa, *Quotes*: https://www.goodreads.com/author/quotes/14958611.Manuela _George_Izunwa (accessed April 16, 2019).

Closing Remarks

1. Richard Rohr, *Growing In Love's Likeness,* Daily Reflections, Saturday, March 31, 2018 (Albuquerque, NM: Center for Action and Contemplation).

2. Thomas Merton, *New Seeds of Contemplation* (New York: New Directions, 1961), 36.

3. Paul Tillich, *The Shaking of the Foundations* (New York: Charles Scribner's Sons, 1948), 182.

ABOUT THE AUTHORS

Dr. Geoff Colvin draws on his experience as a classroom teacher and administrator in both elementary and secondary levels of education; as a researcher and instructor at the University of Oregon; and as a national and international school consultant in the area of behavior disorders. He obtained his Ph.D. from the University of Oregon and has authored and coauthored more than sixty publications in his field, including twelve books. Most recently he published an article in Episcopal Café titled Living with Paradoxes: An Untapped Grace, and has several articles on aspects of contemplative prayer posted on the website for St. Mary's Episcopal Church, Eugene, Oregon. Geoff is now retired, lives with his wife Nola in Eugene, Oregon, devotes time to writing, and is involved with various prayer groups and spiritual studies.

Pat Foley has spent a life-long career in the Catholic educational system, for the most part based in Sydney, Australia. He served as an English teacher, high school principal, and system administrator, mainly in the area of professional development that included managing a program of English and Mathematics inservice for teachers in East Timor. He has Masters Degrees in Arts, Applied Spirituality, and Theology, from the Graduate

Theological Union in Berkeley, University of San Francisco, and University of Sydney, Australia, respectively. Following on from these studies he has worked in the area of spiritual development with teachers and various parish groups. In retirement Pat assists Sudanese refugees with English as a Second Language (ESL), and helps children to develop reading skills. He contributes to the bass line of a local community choir.

What others are saying

"Living with Paradoxes is a valuable take on such common problems (actually opportunities). As a psychologist, I really subscribe to the notion of staying in the tension without premature closure."
—**Pam Birrell**, Ph.D., clinical psychologist, Eugene, Oregon

"I like the whole journey of understanding that this 'in-between' is awkward and begs things of us that really can't resolve the whole situation. This is a very useful and powerful book."
—**Michael Seely**, healthcare executive, Portland, Oregon

"Living with Paradoxes provides a helpful guide to enriching our spiritual seeking."
—**Ron Perry**, counseling psychologist, author of *Empathy—Still at the Heart of Therapy*, Sydney, Australia

"You've done a fine thing in putting together a practical spiritual book. I have been dealing with a particularly difficult paradox of my own and it was helpful to be exposed to the wisdom in *Living with Paradoxes* while trying to navigate my situation."
—**Guy Maynard**, journalist, author of *The Risk of Being Ridiculous*, Eugene, Oregon

"I love the way *Living with Paradoxes* brings together contemporary thinking and mines the whole spiritual journey. I'm keen to try the worksheets, too!"
—**Sarah Foley Massa**, physiotherapist, author of *Matrescence and Spiritual Transformation*, Sydney, Australia

"I found *Living with Paradoxes* to be a most helpful read and very much in tune with some of what I'm experiencing as I try to develop a meditation practice. I often feel like I'm most at peace when I can sit with a sense of not knowing, sort of coming to rest in the indefinite."
—**Alex Granzin**, Ph.D., school psychologist and educational consultant, Springfield, Oregon

74244787R00081

Made in the USA
Columbia, SC
11 September 2019